Architecture of the World

Yves Bottineau
Henri Stierlin (Ed.)

Iberian-American
Baroque

Photos: Yvan Butler

Benedikt Taschen

Editor of Series   Henri Stierlin
Plans   Jean Duret FAS SIA
English Translation   Kenneth Martin Leake

Contents

To Monsieur Victor-L. Tapié
with respect

Introduction

This book covers too vast a field to claim to be even a short history of baroque architecture in the Iberian peninsula. It aims to reveal the basic tendencies of the art with which it is concerned rather than furnish an account of its evolution.

With the help of plans, sections, elevations and photographs accompanied by explanatory notes, the reader will be able to visit a selection of buildings almost unequalled in any other art style. They include the Clerecía at Salamanca with its richly decorated, slim yet powerful tower and its overwhelmingly majestic cloister; the Cartuja at Granada with its wealth of whirling polychrome ornament; the church at Tepotzotlán, its white façade multiplying the shifting rays of the sun, and its altars like gilded grottoes; the palace-monastery of Mafra, its melancholy softened by the undulating lines of the architecture; and the church of São Francisco at Ouro Preto with its well behaved, almost timid charm.

An intelligent reader will immediately characterize all these buildings and similar ones throughout the Iberian peninsular and Latin America as 'baroque'. For they combine dynamic design with superabundant decoration, the well known hallmarks of this term. Nevertheless, it is permissible to doubt the legitimate grounds for such an overall grouping together with the apposite use of the adjective instinctively applied to it. Is it logically in order, in this architectural synthesis, to unite the Spanish and Portuguese worlds into a single artistic universe, and should Spain be studied jointly with her American dominions and Portugal with Brazil? Finally, even if we agree to this simultaneous analysis of buildings scattered over such a vast area from the Mediterranean to the Atlantic and Pacific, can we then qualify as 'baroque' the architecture of these numerous countries, ranging as it does from the first third of the 17th century to the late 18th century, or, in some cases, the early 19th century.

It may be useful, in this preliminary stage of our enquiry, to glance at a similar sphere. With the memory of the great French Gothic cathedrals fixed

Church of San Jorge, La Coruña, Spain (after O. Schubert)

firmly in our minds, let us direct our thoughts to the rest of Europe. Sure enough, we shall find innumerable churches and portals similar in style – at Burgos, Toledo, Leon, Bamberg, Naumburg, Roskilde in Denmark and even at Nicosia in Cyprus. The unity of the Gothic world causes it to surmount indisputable differences and the same applies to the world of the Romanesque. To show a realization of common tendencies and to emphasize them is surely one aspect of a book which will also point out the dissimilarities.

In fact, the universe proposed here has several times been the subject of an overall study. The Spanish art historian, the Marqués de Lozoya, has already

linked the Portuguese world with its dependent territories in the course of a comprehensive survey running to several volumes, and George Kubler and Martin Soria have also published a large book covering the period 1500–1800. Such precedents are sufficient explanation for my undertaking, but there are also additional arguments to justify it. The grouping adhered to in this book does not indicate that the countries under discussion are identical, nor is there any question of transferring the superficially successful dynastic absorption of Portugal by Philip II in 1581 into the realm of architecture. In any case, this was scattered like a bad dream in 1640, and it was not till then that the baroque age began. However strong the differences between Spain and Portugal may have been, not only from the artistic point of view, it must be recognized that their destinies to some extent ran parallel.

It seems natural to link the artistic history of Spain with that of her American possessions. However mindful we may be of the imported nature of this art imposed on Central and South America and however desirous of reading into it the expression of latent nationalism and individual touches stifled by the Conquest, it cannot be denied that it represents to some extent the unity of the Spanish world. It is quite natural to agree with Diego Angulo Iñiguez, the Spanish expert on Spanish-American art, when he writes: 'The buildings on either side of the Atlantic are so closely related that they form a group which is impossible to recognize if one does not know it whole. The American buildings are far from being of exclusive interest to American art historians; they attract Spanish art historians just as much as those of Galicia, Andalusia and Catalonia.' This statement, supported by numerous objective observations, may be confirmed by any visually discerning traveller. Indeed, it is possible to go one step further: the ties between Andalusia and some parts of America are so strong that there sometimes seems less difference between their buildings than between those of Seville, Granada, and Cordova and those of Compostela and elsewhere in Galicia. The shades of difference between the buildings scattered over

Spanish America should not prevent their being studied as a whole, as they have at least one common source – the art of the mother country.

Both pioneer writers of essays, criticism or history such as Eugenio d'Ors, Otto Schubert, Sacheverell Sitwell and Manuel Toussaint and more recent authors have unanimously and instinctively used the word 'baroque' to define the architecture of the

Church of San Francisco, Santiago de Compostela, Spain; façade (after O. Schubert)

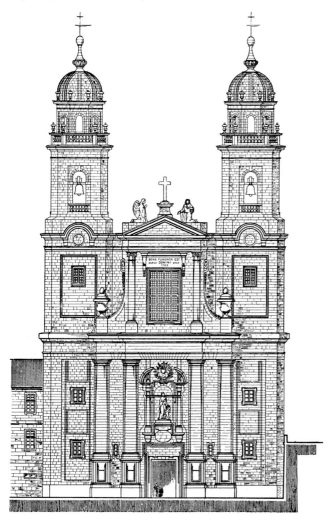

Hispanic world at this period: apparently they considered the richness of the decoration was enough to justify the use of the word. But in 1957 and 1959, George Kubler exercised extreme caution in the use of the term. He refused to apply it generally to the architecture of the 17th and 18th centuries, reserving it for cases where the conception of plan and mass proved similar to buildings which were undoubtedly baroque as in Italian architecture. Such prudence indicative of fine scholarly discipline was not generally noticed.

So the shock was all the more rudely felt in January 1964 when the Centre for Historical and Aesthetic Studies at Caracas under the direction of Graziano Gasparini opened the publication of its bulletin with answers to an 'Enquiry regarding the meaning of Hispano-American baroque architecture'. Experts who had been questioned in America and Europe came forward with a variety of opinions. The majority subscribed to the traditional term and the artistic conception underlying it. George Kubler, however, steadfastly denied the existence of such a thing as Hispano-American baroque architecture.

The following year Graziano Gasparini came wholeheartedly into Kubler's camp. The reasoning leading up to this denial derives from premises which are admissible even though one may reject Gasparini's interpretation. In his opinion, the buildings of Spanish America include only a very small number whose conception of plan and space can be shown as baroque in the real sense of the term. They can only be defined as such by virtue of their decoration which is usually applied to the structure and independent of it. Moreover, in some regions, there are many buildings with very restrained ornamentation. How can one call a group of buildings 'baroque' when they merit this term not for their spatial qualities but on account of their decoration? Nor can they claim this qualification by virtue of their atmosphere, for this is insufficient explanation. If we wish at all costs to rate these buildings as baroque, we must consider them simply as baroque architecture in America, but not American Baroque. On the other hand, the Brazi-

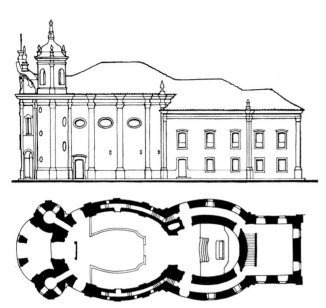

Rosary Chapel, Ouro Preto, 1784: elevation and plan (after Kubler and Soria)

lian churches were not included in the discussion and are classed as authentically baroque.

Finally, in April 1967, Gasparini came out against the chauvinistic interpretation of Baroque in Spanish America; he declared it a complete contradiction of logic that the countries which emerged from the break-up in the 19th century should retrospectively claim the art of the colonial period situated in their respective territories as the expression of their new-found independence. In his opinion such a claim was untenable, as none of these states existed before the emancipation; the buildings erected within their future frontiers mirrored styles which emanated from Madrid, and were therefore part of Spanish colonial art.

The main problems which concern us here – the existence of a baroque architecture in the Iberian peninsular and Central and South America and the question of their interdependence – are not categorically resolved in these pages. The author's sole aim is to attempt an answer by analysis of some typical examples.

The devotees of Baroque did not have time to air their views regarding these difficulties before they were confronted with yet another, this time centring round South German 18th century architecture. In 1966, Philippe Minguet in a study devoted to this subject declared that Rococo was not merely a sub-division of Baroque, but an autonomous artistic and historical period. When news of this study and its conclusions reached the ears of historians of Spain, Portugal, and their possessions, they were bound to wonder about its application to their own work. Should the proposed separation of the two arts in Southern Germany be applied to the far vaster dominion of the Iberian peninsula and Latin America? This book must also make a modest contribution on this score, attempting to find a way amid these new found theories.

As fresh light is constantly being shed on our chosen subject, it is all the more necessary to give a careful explanation of the plan of this book. It demonstrates in stages why, how, and to what extent, the architecture under discussion is truly baroque. The first chapter outlines the historical background; this does not of its own accord decide the nature of buildings but may, to a certain extent, explain them. We must also decide whether this really was a background capable of producing baroque art. Emotive contact with some of the key buildings reproduced in the plates will recreate the impression of their size and space; but stylistic problems will be dealt with in the second chapter. The third chapter deals with stylistic analysis and the conception of architecture, together with the main principles of plan and mass; stress is laid on the links between structure and decoration. This analysis proposes a primary solution to the problem whether an Iberian and Ibero-American baroque architecture really exists. Chapter 4 is devoted to decoration, its iconography and the unity and diversity of its motifs, and contributes to the conclusions of the previous chapter. Chapter 5 examines the problem of the baroque feeling for space around its buildings and in its town planning, and rounds off the approach offered by the book.

1. Historical Background

Iberian and Ibero-American architecture is linked both directly and indirectly to the economics of the 17th and 18th centuries. On the other hand, political, social and religious conditions are usually considered distinguishing features of the Baroque without being determining factors.

Baroque and economics

The mass and extent of buildings depend on economic conditions, as a period of prosperity obviously possesses greater resources for creating architecture than a poor one. These conditions help to explain certain directions taken in the arts, but they have only produced a limited effect on architecture, notably in a change of form.

Thanks to the treasures of America the 16th century had been a period of expansion. Portugal had reached the peak of its fortunes under Manuel I and John III. Spain, enriched by the precious metals sent from the West Indies in the reigns of Charles V and Philip II, attempted to impose her conception of a Catholic Europe dominated by the Hapsburgs over the entire continent.

In the 17th century, however, the states of the Spanish Crown which up to 1640 included Portugal as the result of dynastic union, experienced a sharp and cruel depression. The favourable balance of the economy was overturned in 1605–13, and in 1623–50 there was severe depression, followed by heavy inflation between 1664 and 1680. The state became bankrupt four times in fifty years – in 1607, 1627, 1647, and 1656. The execrable tax system which varied in each region, only increased the economic difficulties. The population of Spain had increased in the 16th century, but from this time on depopulation started to create havoc as the result of emigration to the Indies, an abundance of clergy, and the expulsion of the Moriscoes in 1609–14. There may be argument about the exact figures and scope of the movement, but the general outline is only too clear. Castile suffered especially, while Catalonia and the eastern provinces more or less escaped the disaster on account of their

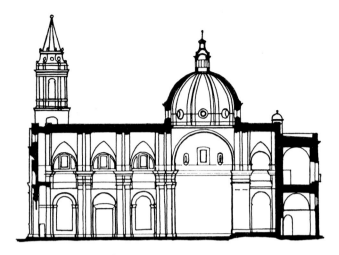

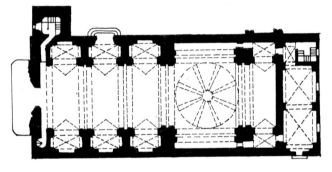

Church at Umbrete, by Diego Antonio Diaz, 1725–1733:
façade, section and plan (after Kubler and Soria)

own financial resources. The Portuguese also suffered severely from the backwash of the difficulties experienced by the crown to which they were linked, both at home and in their overseas dominions, where the attacks of the Dutch succeeded in the temporary conquest of part of Brazil (1624–54). Home, foreign and economic problems were completely intermingled. The capture by the Dutch of the fleet of New Spain with 80 tons of silver at Matanzas on the 7th and 8th September 1628 was a disaster for the entire Iberian peninsula. There followed the revolt of Catalonia and Portugal in 1640 and the French victories which culminated in the Treaty of the Pyrenees in 1659 – events which transcribed into military and

diplomatic terms a collapse that had its original roots in the sphere of economics.

This collapse can be explained as due to the tensions induced by wars and colonization and to errors such as the expulsion of the Moors. Its effects, however, may have been more limited than have long been believed. Indeed, it is insufficient to recall that the treasure of America, instead of being converted into durable investments, passed to Spain for the sole purpose of financing the wars of Charles V and Philip II. It must be stressed to what extent Spanish decadence was caused by false social and economic concepts bred of recent triumphs; these included an obsession with purity of blood and a refusal to undertake certain manual or industrial tasks, which engendered widespread inactivity.

The late 17th century, however, introduced a fresh, contrasting outlook which became firmly established in the 18th century. Henceforward, there was less disturbance from armed conflict, and events grew less dramatic in character. Europe passed into a period of expansion, and a portion of society was able to live a life of relative ease. Two basic factors permitted the recovery of the Spanish economy: the change in administrative technique, thanks to the ministers of the new dynasty established by Philip V, the first of the Bourbons, and the activities of the outlying regions of Catalonia, the eastern provinces, and Andalusia. Portugal had enjoyed the riches of Brazil, but wasted them on sumptuary expenditure, thus repeating in the 18th century the mistake made previously by Spain. Reform of the economy did not take place until 1750–77 under the ministry of Pombál.

The mistakes and subsequent reforms of these two centuries may again be noted to a lesser extent in America.

As the result of the 'colonial pact', the economy of the American colonies was exclusively directed to the profit of the mother country. This was, however, considerably corrected by smuggling and piracy especially on the part of the English in the 18th century to the detriment of the government in Madrid; in Brazil correction was due to the liberalism of the authorities. Thus completely different results were arrived at in Portuguese and Spanish America.

In 17th century Brazil the mining industry was still at the prospecting stage, and the booming economy was that of an agricultural country whose staple crop was sugar up to 1680. The sugar production of the Antilles brought an end to the prosperity of the Portuguese colony, but it revived with the mines. From 1720–25 the production of gold and diamonds was marked by an extraordinary advance together with the development of the region of Minas Geraes where towns sprang up at Mariana, Ouro Preto, Sabara, and São João d'El Rei.

In the 17th and 18th centuries the population and economy of Spanish America were at a standstill, and it has often been said that the silver mines started

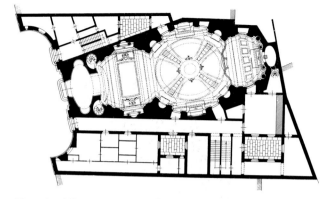

Church of San Marcos, Madrid: plan (after O. Schubert)

to decline. The truth, however, is not so simple. The mines of New Spain did not regain their prosperity, but fresh veins were discovered at San Luis Potosi (1614–29), Chihuahua (1630–32) and in New Galicia (1672). In Peru extraction developed to an even greater extent at Oruro (1595–1606), Pasco (1630), Laicaota (1657), and Huantajaya. In fact, the huge area making up Spanish America underwent a period of consolidation after the brilliance of the 16th century.

This economic outline suggests certain findings in the realms of art and, more especially, of architecture.

In time of war or financial difficulties it is quite usual for commissions to become fewer and for their execution to be interrupted. Examples of this can even be quoted from the 18th century and the following may be found in R.C. Taylor's study of Francisco Hurtado. On 13th February 1718, Antonio Gomez, the treasurer of the Cartuja at Granada, wrote a vehement, picturesquely phrased letter to his superior at Madrid: 'I am writing to you in the guise of a lowing heifer, hungry for money; for there is very little left in our coffers; which is a great pity as it hinders work on our chapel'. The sacristy of the cathedral at Granada, designed by Hurtado, also remained incomplete for a long time for lack of resources.

The double comparison between the depression of the 17th century and the tense nature of the Baroque, and between 18th century expansion and the relaxed

Sagrario of Granada Cathedral: plan (after O. Schubert)

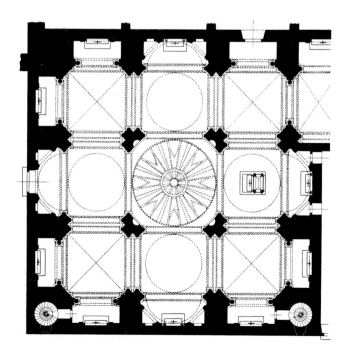

optimism of the Rococo from 1700 to about 1760, is also well known.

Leaving the general evolution of art to one side, we may wonder whether economics may help us to establish more exact period divisions. This is unlikely, however, for several reasons. The rhythms of economics and of stylistic renewal as established for 17th and 18th century Spain are seen to be quite independent of one another. Basic changes in style took place between 1600 and 1630, 1640 and 1680, and from 1700 onwards, and these developments cannot be associated with decisive dates outside the world of art. In Spanish America the whole development of baroque architecture took place during a period of stagnation.

Even if there are several cases where there are clearly links between economics and architecture,

the former does not explain the style of the latter. The Spanish clergy received their revenues in kind and were sheltered from the ups and downs of money like the great landed proprietors; sometimes they could build when the king was not in a position to do so. The financial troubles of 1650–60 resulted in more commissions for decoration and fewer for actual building. In 1662 Brother Lorenzo of San Nicolás wrote: 'Today Spain and the other provinces are in no position to undertake the construction of large buildings, but can only preserve existing ones.' The luxurious palaces of the Portuguese kings were due to the treasures of America, and these treasures also provided the 'mineros', the exploiters of the mines of Mexico and Peru, with the means to build magnificent churches. Why was it, however, that the wealth of the Spanish clergy, the Portuguese court, and the 'mineros' resulted in the erection of buildings in the baroque style rather than any other?

Church of San Marcos, Madrid: cross-section and longitudinal section (after O. Schubert)

8

Similar puzzling questions may arise over the richness of the altars. The reason is quite clear at Santa Prisca in Taxco and the Valenciana in New Spain, as both these churches were built by 'mineros'. Why, on the other hand, does the Baroque at Guanajuato not equal the display of the nearby Valenciana, and why does it attain such richness in the churches and palaces of Puebla so far away from the mines? The altars of Mexico evoke gold, but it was silver that was produced by the mines of New Spain. Finally, in Brazil, whose wealth was founded on gold, overloaded decoration of this metal was not used in the province of Minas Geraes, but from the late 17th century in Bahia, Recife and Rio de Janeiro, none of which produced precious metals.

In these cases, it is impossible to explain the choice of a style by reference to economics; it must be sought through the influence of other factors, political, social, and religious. These go to make up a complex whole which may be termed collective psychology and its connections with baroque architecture are emphatically convincing.

Baroque and collective psychology

As we have learnt from the works of Victor L. Tapié, in general terms Baroque is a translation of the psychology of monarchical Catholic countries and feudal rural societies fond of fashioning or contemplating a world of glory, imagination and sensitivity where decoration plays the lead. Such was certainly the case with Iberian and Ibero-American architecture in the 17th and 18th centuries.

The monarchy of the Ancien Régime was synonymous with show and state display. All the royal houses shared these common tendencies which, with the consent of public opinion, were more marked in France than in the Iberian peninsular. At Versailles the sovereign appeared as God's anointed, the first gentleman of his realm, the master surrounded, since the time of Louis XIV, by a tamed nobility.

This picture must be modified where Spain is concerned. Kings were not considered divine as in France. The 17th century Hapsburgs did not rival Louis XIV's anxiety for display; etiquette and devotion to some extent took the place of majesty and Philip III let himself be guided by a meticulous sense of piety. Philip IV was an enlightened connoisseur who loved festivities and the arts for their own sakes without worrying too much about their political significance; Louis XIV, on the other hand, was also naturally inclined towards them, but bent them to serve the prestige of the throne. Charles II too often suffered ill health to be the centre of a festive court and was sometimes even too poor to have a proper guard at his command, so could never rival the French king. Nevertheless, the basic principle at Madrid and Versailles remained the same: the king had to appear surrounded by an imposing court in conformity with the rules of strict protocol in palaces worthy of the crown, the centre of impressive ceremonial. Repeated criticisms directed against 17th century sovereigns over the cost of their establishments serve as proof that this principle was widely applied. When the Duc d'Anjou, grandson of Louis XIV, became Philip V in 1700, Spain adopted the French conception of the monarchy, though with reduced brilliance. This conception held firm even when the new king was struggling against severe nervous collapse, and was also respected by his sons, Ferdinand VI and Charles III.

Spanish America was never visited by any of its sovereigns, but knew of royal splendour through the viceroys and captains-general, important personages with an elegant train of subordinates. The viceroyalties of New Spain and Peru supported real courts at Mexico City and Lima; to these were added in the 18th century, New Granada, established temporarily from 1717 to 1723 and permanently in 1739, and Rio de la Plata in 1776 with Buenos Aires as capital. The captains-general were established over Guatemala, Chile, Venezuela from 1731, and Cuba from 1764.

The luxury and bigotry of the 18th century Portuguese kings is justly notorious for the contrast between their small kingdom and the prodigality they were able to exercise thanks to the treasures of Brazil.

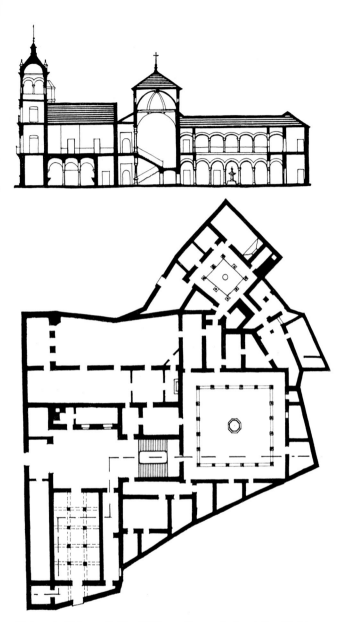

Valverde Palace, Ecija, 1756: section and plan (after Kubler and Soria)

Another reason for this splendour lay in dynastic rivalry. Pedro II, husband of Maria Sophia of Neuburg, was brother-in-law to Charles II and Leopold I; John V was brother-in-law to the Emperor Charles VI through Queen Mariana, and Joseph I to Ferdinand VI and Charles III of Spain through his sister Barbara and his wife Mariana Victoria. The governor-general of Brazil was first stationed at Bahia and then went on to Rio de Janeiro, becoming viceroy in 1763. The captain-generalcies, the chief of which were at Pernambuco (1657), São Paulo (1706) and Minas Geraes (1720) were directly dependent on the Lisbon government. The holders of all these positions, in a colony on the other side of the Atlantic which derived its wealth from mining and sugar, were equipped with all that was needed to reflect the royal splendour.

In 17th century Spain 95 per cent of the land was owned either by the king, the nobility or the clergy. The peasants who made up the vast majority of the nation were dominated by the nobility, a few bishops and archbishops, and the religious orders. The more ostentatious noblemen, holders of one or more titles, lived surrounded by hordes of servants and so-called clients who gave a striking impression of their power; they possessed unique financial resources which kept them virtually remote from economic difficulties. The same could be said of the better provided prelates and religious orders. This outline of a society with wealth derived from the land remained valid throughout the 18th century despite the slight differences brought about by the start of industrialization. The inhabitants of the kingdom took pleasure in the Baroque; some commissioned and paid for works of art which others could only enjoy with startled eyes.

An identical outline emerged for Spanish America, though here it united different races. The Indians were conscripted into labour forces ('encomiendas') and were allowed to be exploited by their Spanish masters on condition that the latter undertook their religious conversion, though this was seldom insisted upon; the labour forces disappeared in the late 17th century but survived in other guises. In this way a class of great landowners came into being, to the gain of the creoles and whiter half-castes; to these can be added the senior clergy and the religious orders, as in Spain, by virtue of their estates. It was these landowners who commissioned the masterpieces of colonial baroque architecture, and the Indians, enclosed both in their traditional hierarchies and in the new ones resulting from the conquest, were invited to gaze on them. Deprived of their past culture and even providing the labour force, they brought to the Baroque their strong, innocent emotions and their sense of luxuriant decoration, though they were, of course, as ignorant of the name of this type of architecture as the peasants of Europe.

There was a similar population distribution in Portugal and Brazil: peasants and an aristocracy of nobles and clergy. In Brazil, however, the country societies were markedly patriarchal and endowed with special features due to the slave trade. In Africa, these slaves had enjoyed a cultural level superior to that of the Indians and they assimilated the Christian civilization of their white masters to a remarkable degree; they impregnated it with their temperamental qualities and were the originators of the mulattos who were wonderfully gifted in the sphere of the arts, as can be seen from the masterpieces of Aleijadinho in Minas Geraes.

From the mass of Indians encircled by the landed proprietors we may turn, in our pursuit of an atmosphere favourable to the Baroque, to the admirable, often heroic work of the utopistic Jesuits in their missions. Known in Spanish America as 'reductions' and in Brazil as 'aldeiamentos' each mission formed a world apart, linked to exploitation of the earth but also affording a taste of divine ordinance in its hierarchical and topographical arrangement, particularly in their beautiful church interiors.

This survey of connections between Baroque and society cannot be complete without some reflections on the city merchants and the mine owners. As they were used to objective considerations and concerned with strict calculations, we should expect to find them leaders of a type of classicism translating the start of industrialization and middle class capitalism into terms of art.

This seems a tricky problem, but can quite well be resolved provided we accept an extension of basic ideas. In other words, we must conjure up the ties between the Baroque and mercantile activity. There is, however, some ambiguity in the case of the rebuilding of Lisbon by Pombál after the 1755 earthquake. Was its restrained style due to the influence of the taste of the merchants in the minister's immediate circle or was it merely caused by the economics, planning and functional outlook exacted by such a large-scale undertaking? Did the merchants moderate the style of architecture or were they themselves restrained by the needs of the rebuilding? In any case, there exists a baroque style common to the Mediterranean ports of Genoa, Toulon and Valencia, so why should we be amazed by the Baroque of Vera Cruz and the Brazilian coast? It has been proved that baroque towns like Lecce in Apulia were the seats of religious orders owning land in the regions concerned. Undoubtedly, Puebla with its many churches and monasteries was in the same category. Finally, the merchants and mine owners naturally gravitated towards the Baroque for obvious reasons – because they wanted to publicize themselves and this style constituted a universal architectural language, used

Pocito Chapel, Guadalupe, Mexico: elevation

Festival of the fifth centenary of the Reconquest, at Valencia, 1738. Altar of the convent of the Merced

primarily by the Spanish and Portuguese Church, with manifold shades of meaning.

In this collective psychology the intensity of Catholic feeling must have been at least as powerful as the tendencies we have just reviewed.

Spain was the chosen country of the Counter-Reformation, which developed without making a break with medieval religious feeling. The old established, reformed or new orders like the Jesuits gained astonishing impetus from it, and the action of the brotherhoods strengthened the work of the lay and regular clergy. The Council of Trent extolled the cults of the Eucharist, the Virgin and the saints and the practice of pilgrimages. The ceremonies pertaining to the Corpus Christi procession, the Semana Santa, and patronal festivals were repeated annually, taking up several days each month, and there were also canonizations. This type of religious feeling was both ecstatic and deep-seated, based on outward show and inward emotion, sensual and dogmatic. It could be termed popular, but first and foremost it appealed to the Hispanic temperament.

On its arrival in America, Spanish catholicism developed rapidly, thanks to the action of the religious orders, which proselytized the Indians with exemplary zeal. In the course of the 16th century the clergy who came from Europe were inclined to harbour illusions regarding the assimilation of these new Christian children. In the 17th century, however, the clergy were strict on dogma, did not consider the natives suitable for the priesthood, and kept them in a state of spiritual underdevelopment. The Catholic faith with its countless monasteries, brotherhoods and ceremonies, continued to pursue a many-sided passionate life to some extent marred by pagan superstitions and survivals, but undeniably powerful and sincere. The most famous of its forms of worship was, and still is, that which made the Virgin of Guadalupe, who appeared to the Indian, Juan Diego, in 1531, the patron both of Mexico and the whole of Spanish America. There were also countless other pilgrimages which resulted in the building of magnificent or purely moving sanctuaries. In Brazil Catholicism ensured the unity of a heterogeneous population; under the tropical sky it especially inflamed the Africans and mulattos with a passionate ardour probably never equalled in Portugal.

The various factors analysed in the course of this chapter are sufficient proof that, by virtue of its historical background, 17th and 18th century Iberian and Ibero-American architecture can be classed as Baroque.

Plates

Braga

17 Staircases rising towards the church. The pilgrimage of the Bom Jesus is basically a reconstruction of Golgotha enlarged by baroque devotion to cover the story of human redemption. Its present state includes a major portion of the original 18th-century features such as the Staircase of the Five Senses despite transformations dating from the end of the century (Cruz Amarante's church) and from the 19th century (the Staircase of the Theological Virtues).

18 Detail of 17.

19 Shell fountain. Water symbolizing the blood of Christ flows from it through the Saviour's five wounds.

20 Chapel on the Patio of the Evangelists.

Mafra

21 The church in the centre of the principal façade. The palace and monastery of Mafra was built in 1717 by Ludovice for John V, and the bulbous spires of the towers recall buildings in Germany and Italy.

22 Principal façade. Mafra recalls the Escorial by reason of its imposing dimensions, but there the resemblance ends.

23 Belfry of the church. Its design bears resemblance to details at the Clerecía in Salamanca.

24 The monastery garden. In the background, the church.

25 Dome of the church.

26 The library.

27 Detail of the library. The stucco decorations of the galleries and ceiling were executed by the Augustinian Canons (1777–1791). The rococo style here is brittle and broken up.

28 Chapter hall.

29 Detail of chapter hall.

Rio de Janeiro

30 São Bento, the nave of the church. This Benedictine monastery provides material for the study of the development of the 'talha' in the Brazilian capital in the course of the 17th and 18th centuries. The work in the nave was entrusted to the lay 'entalhador' Alessandro Machado Pereira in 1717; he was commissioned to complete it in 15 years. The pillar statues of Fathers of the Church, kings and emperors were executed by José da Conceição da Silva and Simão da Cunha.

31 The nave looking towards the 'capela mór'. The 'talha' of the 'capela' was reworked by the 'entalhador' Inácio Ferreiro Pinto (1787–1794).

32 Detail of the nave. Fathers of the Church.

33 Detail of nave arcade.

34 Sacristy; built (1669–1673) and vaulted (1673–1676) by Fray Bernardo de São Bento Correa de Sousa.

35 Altar of the sacristy (1714–1717).

Ouro Preto

36 São Francisco de Asis, façade. This chapel was built between 1766 and 1794. The frontispiece and the sculptures are by Aleijadinho.

37 Detail of the façade. The curving movement of the walls, the window surrounds, and the recession of the lateral towers are highly idiosyncratic.

38 High altar by Aleijadinho. Executed after a project of 1778–1779, it reveals the artist as an interpreter of the Rococo and a connoisseur of architectural shapes more subtle than those of the façade.

39 Detail of paintings on nave ceiling; executed by Manuel da Costa Ataíde in accordance with a contract of 1801, on the theme of the Immaculate Conception.

40 Detail.

Palace-monastery of Mafra (Portugal)
Plan 1:2000

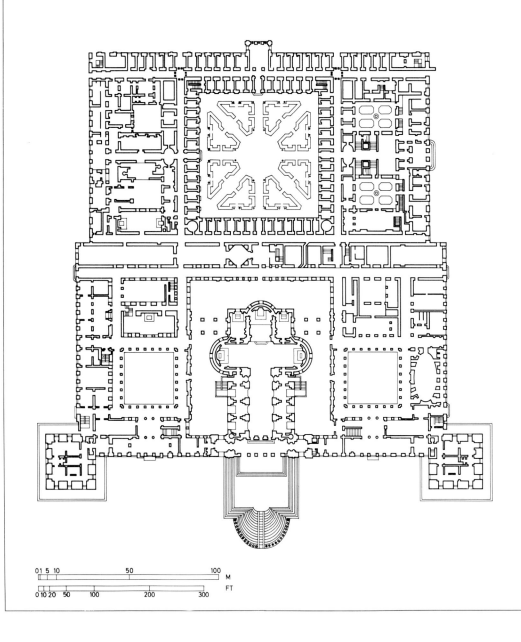

0 1 5 10   50   100 M

0 10 20 50   100   200   300 FT

Church of São Francisco de Asis, Ouro Preto (Brazil)
Section and plan 1:300

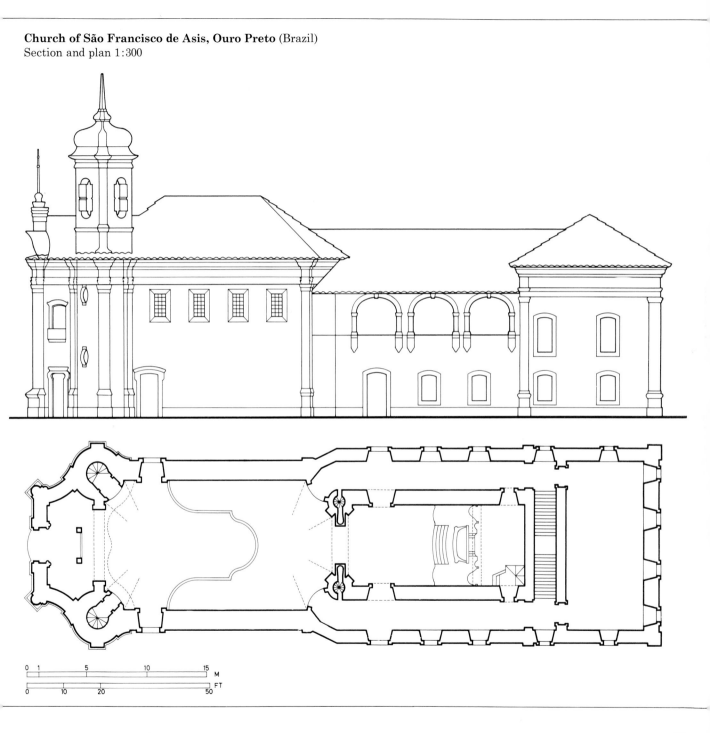

0 1   5   10   15
|————————————————————————————————| M
0   10   20   50
|————————————————————————————————| FT

Notes

Braga

Bom Jesus do Monte. The Monte Espinho near Braga has been the scene of a pilgrimage of the Holy Cross since the 14th century, but it attained its culminating point, both artistically and doctrinally, through the agency of the Bishop of Braga, Dom Rodrigo de Moura Telles who endowed the site with an iconographic programme stemming from both pagan and religious sources and dedicated to the story of Calvary and the Redemption. This scheme was carried out in several stages and continued after the prelate's death. It included the entrance portico, the road known as the 'Via Crucis' with its chapels, the staircase of the Five Senses, some fountains and an elliptically planned church. In 1767, the generosity of Manuel Rebelo da Costa led to the installation of the patio of the Evangelists with the fountains dedicated to them and the chapels consecrated to the Apparition of Christ to Mary, the pilgrims of Emmaeus and the Ascension; this patio formed the end of the spiritual journey of the pilgrimage. The ruinous state of the church resulted in its destruction and replacement by another building of quadrangular plan on a site further up the hill. In the 19th century the staircase of the Five Senses was extended towards the sanctuary by the staircase of the Theological Virtues and the majority of the chapels on the 'Via Crucis' were rebuilt.

Mafra

Mafra was founded by John V who wished God to provide him with an heir. The building was designed by Ludovice (Johann Friedrich Ludwig) who, instead of taking the Escorial as his model, preferred to find prototypes in Germany and Italy where he had worked. The undertaking was started in 1717 and was only brought to a successful conclusion with the help of Brazilian gold. The church was consecrated on October 22, 1733, but its real completion dates from after 1770. The main inspiration for its architecture comes from Italy and it is decorated with statues from the same country; it occupies the centre of the façade while the monastery which was first in the care of Franciscans and then of Augustinian Canons is pushed back to the rear. The palace is situated in the front portion of the building. This whole layout dissociates Mafra from the Escorial and relates it to German and Italian architecture.

Rio de Janeiro

São Bento. The installation of the Benedictines in Brazil, at São Salvador, dates from 1581. The monastery of São Bento at Rio was founded five years later. In 1617–1618, Francisco de Frias da Mesquita, chief constructional engineer of the colony, produced plans for the first rebuilding of the church and monastery; but because of the war with Holland, these were not realized for a very long time. The roof of the nave was not set in position until 1666–1669. The plans received fresh impetus from 1668 onwards, thanks to Fray Bernardo de São Bento Correa de Sousa, a former military engineer, who had entered the Benedictine Order after the death of his wife. After the production of a plan in 1668 which was considered too expensive, he executed another which he offered in 1670 and, between this date and his death in 1693, he completed the church and built the sacristy. The monks then devoted themselves to the building of the monastery which was completed in 1755 in accordance with a plan of 1684. The 'talha' was also executed in stages: 1669–1673, the church doors and the stalls in the 'coro'; 1682–1688, the balustrades of the galleries by Frei Domingos da Conceição; 1690, 'talha' of the 'arco cruzeiro' by the same hand; 1717, contract drawn up with Alessandro Machado Pereira to execute the wooden sculpture of the nave in fifteen years; 1714–1717, the sacristy altar; 1734, contract for the 'talha' in the two chapels at the entrance to the nave; 1739–1743, 'talha' in the 'coro'; c. 1747–c. 1772, side altars in the aisles; 1760–1769, 'talha' of the reliquary chapel on the first floor of the monastery; 1787–1794, new 'talha' for the 'capela mór' (and the sacristy); 1795–1800, building and 'talha' of the large chapel of the Holy Sacrament. (Chronology–Germain Bazin).

Ouro Preto

São Francisco de Asis. Doubts over the part played by Aleijadinho in the building and decoration of this chapel of the Third Order of St Francis are due to the loss of certain documents and the fact that, being a mulatto, he could not be a contracting party. It appears that he altered the façade in accordance with his plan of 1774 and executed the high altar after a project of 1778. These two dates merely constitute points of reference in a slow, complex undertaking in which other hands intervened. Study of the building reveals Aleijadinho as an architect with an aptitude for measured harmony and an altar sculptor with a marked taste for the rococo style.

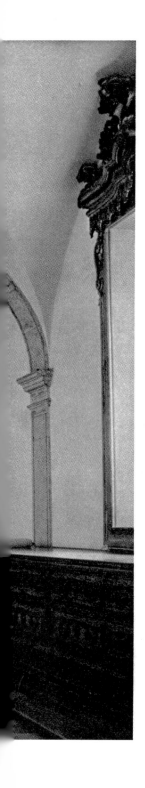

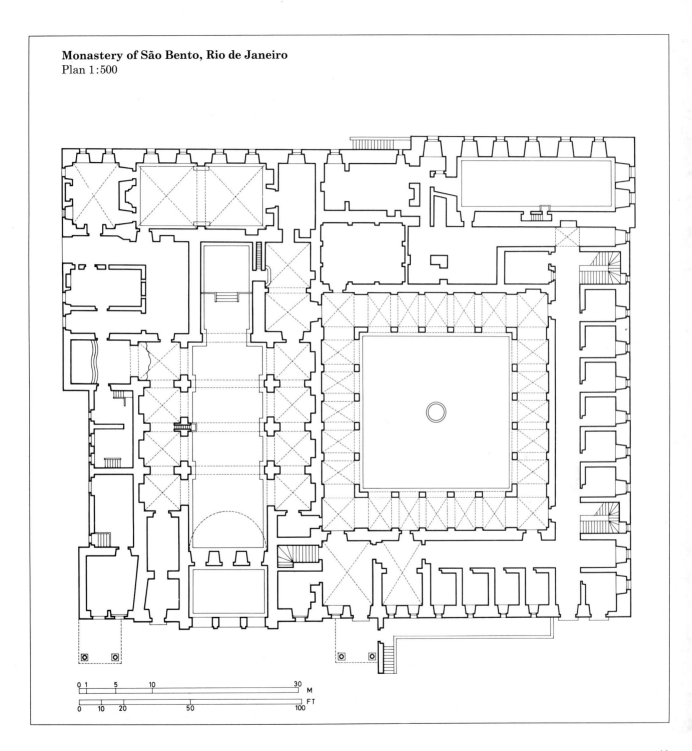

Monastery of São Bento, Rio de Janeiro
Plan 1:500

0 1 5   10   30 M

0   10 20   50   100 FT

Cathedral of the Pilar, Saragossa
Plan and section 1:1000
Detail of the Chapel of the Pilar: Plan 1:333

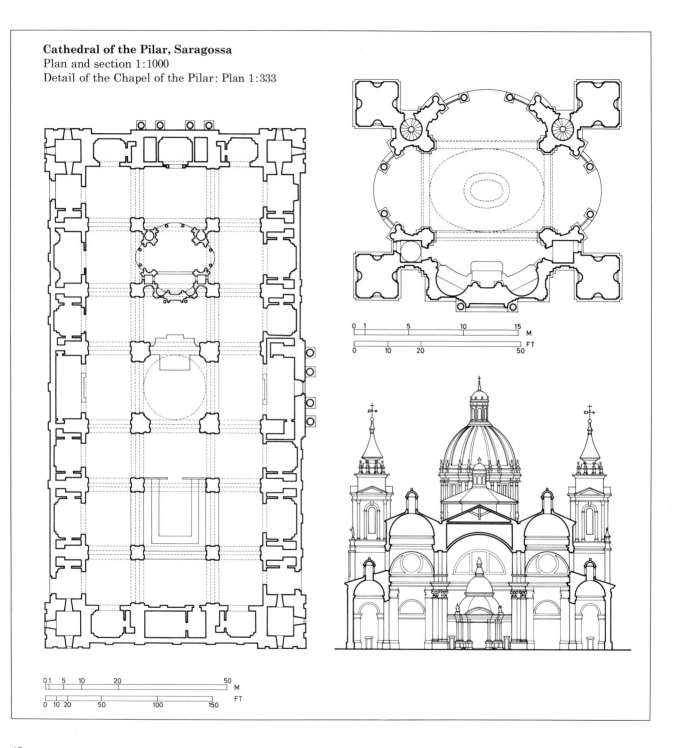

0 1   5   10   20   50
                                                              M
0   10 20   50   100   150
                                                              FT

0 1 5   10   20   50
                                              M
0   10 20   50   100   150
                                              FT

2. Visual Perception and Artistic Originality

The logical build-up of this book needs, at this point, an intermediate stage. We should make a new approach, leave aside all considerations of style and make acquaintance with a few key buildings reproduced for our pleasure and visual analysis in the plates.

Salamanca: Clerecía

The visitor to Salamanca who catches a general view of the town from the Calle de Fonseca or, further away, from the southern end of the Roman bridge, will be struck by a building of imposing, almost overwhelming, dimensions with sharp horizontal lines. This is the Clerecía, the former College of the Jesuits.

On careful examination these masses fall apart. The vast rectangular buildings, with every second storey marking a horizontal division and their summits lightened by a gallery, house a succession of cells. The upper portions of the church also stand out – the dome over the centre of the transept, and the two bells towers on the façade.

If we approach the lofty walls of these buildings, the originality of their surfaces will be confirmed. Cornices, pilasters, and the surrounds of attic and lower windows, are all as plain as possible, forming a bare, geometrical, though remarkably compact, network over the severe face of the College.

The richness of the church façade increases with height. The pairs of Corinthian columns and the cornices of the first two levels are both architecture and decoration; they effortlessly accommodate the sumptous cartouches with the royal arms in the divisions demarcated by them. Above the balustrade, the belfries and the attic of the central section break out in a profusion of obliquely set massive columns, pinnacles, statues and decorative sculptures; this abundance, its beauty enhanced by the golden colour of the stone, gains full significance if we admire the upper portions of the façade from the patio of the Casa de las Conchas, a neighbouring building of lesser height.

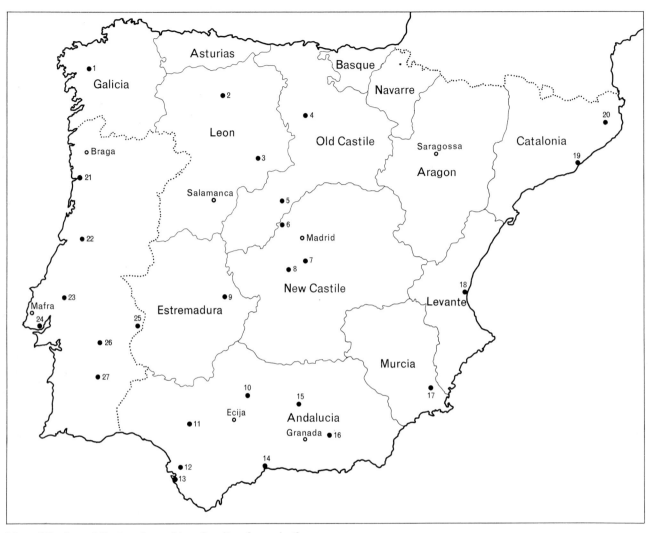

Map of Spain and Portugal, marking the sites shown in the
photographs in this book, together with the chief places
mentioned in the text:

1 Santiago de Compostela	9 Guadalupe	17 Murcia	25 Elvas
2 Leon	10 Cordova	18 Valencia	26 Evora
3 Valladolid	11 Seville	19 Barcelona	27 Beja
4 Burgos	12 Jerez de la Frontera	20 Gerona	
5 Segovia	13 Cadiz	21 Oporto	
6 Escorial	14 Malaga	22 Coimbra	
7 Aranjuez	15 Jaen	23 Santarem	
8 Toledo	16 Guadix	24 Lisbon	

The church interior is made up of straight-forward sections – nave and side chapels, transept and magnificently luminous dome, the surroundings of the high altar and, beyond, the monks' choir. The elegant decoration flows over this simple structure – sculptured stone covering the flutings of pilasters, the divisions of the vaulting and the reliefs of the dome. Golden retables glow at intervals lit by the flames of candles and fitful rays of light.

The vast patio impresses through its rather heavy splendour and projecting columns in front of a two-tiered arcade which catch the eye. They support a third storey, lower but just as richly decorated, below a row of small pyramids.

Such is the Clerecía. It stays in the mind by virtue of its logical overall composition, its monumentality, and the subtlety of rich rectilinear decoration.

Granada: Cartuja

In his 'Voyage en Espagne' (1850), Théophile Gautier reveals his fascination for the decoration of the Cartuja at Granada. In his own words 'The decoration of this church is extraordinary; it consists of stucco arabesques executed in accordance with a really amazing variety of motifs. It would appear that the architect intended to compete in complex lightness, but in completely different taste, with the lacework tracery of the Alhambra. In this vast interior there is not a hand's width uncovered by flowers, imitation damask, leaves, tooling or tufts like cabbage hearts; anyone wanting to make an accurate sketch of it would be driven mad. The choir is faced with porphyry and precious marbles'.

Contemporary visitors are subject to the same general impression: amazement before such a symphony of colour. On the other hand, they will probably find Gautier's comparison with the Alhambra more literary than objective despite the care with which he advances it.

The contemporary visitor will especially regret that Gautier took no notice of space or volume, probably because he was blinded by the decoration which pleased him in his double role of poet and critic of painting. The plan of the 16th century church is very simple, with a single nave and concerns us solely on account of the chancel separating the monks' choir from that of the lay brothers and the abundance of the stucco motifs. The Sagrario, on the other hand, cannot be reduced to a lavish arrangement of statues and columns, an abundance of colours and rich materials; a lofty tabernacle rises up under the frescoed dome and the result is a continual surprise of new volumes. Finally, the irregular bays of the sacristy with their subtly varied rhythm lead up to the wide, oval dome which enlarges and highlights the volumes in front of the rear altar.

Seville: San Luis

The façade of San Luis, church of the former novitiate of the Jesuits, is set between unremarkable buildings in a narrow, crowded Seville street close to San Gil, home of the famous Virgin de la Macarena. We are brought up sharp by its brick walls and our eyes are attracted to the ornamentation covering the fluted columns, the pilasters, and the pediments of the lower storey, which contrast with the almost plain brick surfaces. It needs an effort to raise one's eyes to the upper storey which is less richly ornamented as the full splendour of the decoration is concentrated on the Solomonic columns and lofty curved pediment of the central section. Unfortunately, it is difficult to grasp the outlines of the polygonal towers with their alternating windows and niches and their brick –covered domes. Nevertheless, careful inspection reveals a balanced composition hiding beneath the magnificent decoration. The great central door with its semicircular arch is separated from two other lower doors, surmounted by small windows, by a pair of fluted columns. There are also two doors at the bases of the towers, arched like the centre door but not so high; these are framed by pairs of pilasters. The rhythm of pilasters and columns is repeated in the storey above; there is also a similar rhythm of openings, but these take the form of lofty rectangular windows with triangular or inward curving pediments.

This synthesis of lavish decoration and complex construction is even more accentuated within, where it encompasses both wall surfaces and spatial layout. At first the eye is lost amid the gold, the paintings, the retables reaching to the summits of the arches, the multiplicity of vast niches, and the hemispheric volumes. On careful examination, however, the church imposes a feeling of grandeur mingled with a sensation of airiness. Four large chapels, one of which serves as a passage from the entrance side, alternate with four smaller, lower chapels. All are built to a semicircular plan, are separated by Solomonic columns and set beneath a dome the size of which

Map of Mexico and Central America:

1 Guadalajara	9 Vera Cruz
2 Aguas Calientes	10 Oaxaca
3 San Luis Potosí	11 Mérida
4 San Miguel de Allende	12 Antigua
5 Salamanca	13 Guatemala City
6 Mexico City	14 San Salvador
7 Tepotzotlán	15 Havana
8 Puebla	16 Santiago de Cuba

is increased by its bold conception and light effects so that it seems to float like a heavenly saucer. Retables, statues and doors increase the decorative richness, whilst the galleries happily create areas of clarity beneath their light arches.

The private chapel of the novitiate in the earlier monastery buildings is completely different in conception and contrasts with the ordering of plan and volumes in the church. It comprises a single nave the importance of which lies in the beauty of its decoration. This surrounds the paintings set in the side walls, breaks over the vaults and surrounds the centrally placed altar with its graceful profusion.

In short, San Luis at Seville rivals in subtlety the Cartuja at Granada.

Tepotzotlán (Mexico)

Some 40 kilometres north of Mexico City, on the road linking the capital with Querétaro, our attention is attracted by the beauty of a natural terrace in the centre of a vast plain bordered by distant mountains. Here stand the buildings of Tepotzotlán, one of the most famous of the Jesuit foundations in the New

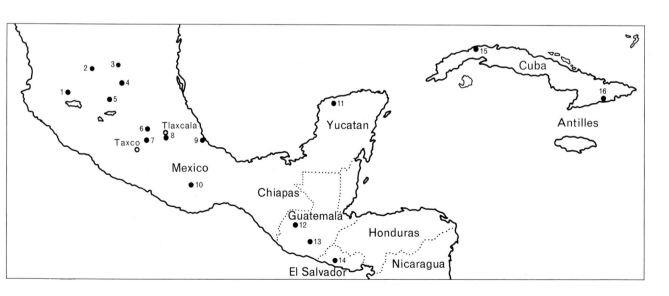

World. They include the church, the college of the Indians and the novitiate, which now form the Museum of the Viceroyalty, the Mexican colonial period. Travelling over the wide landscape with its green vegetation, the visitor may guide himself by the church's single tower. Once past the austere side door, he will enter the wide square and atrium in front of the monastery.

The recently cleaned façade, outlined white against the sky, now faces him. On the right, the tower accentuates the forceful uplift of the composition. The diffuse sculpture of the central section reaches the cap of the tower, then rises and descends again on to its curvilinear top. It is vigorously distributed over the belfry whilst the lower stages of the tower are only studded with bosses – and this arrangement of the soaring sculpture increases the building's strong feeling of ascension. The structure made up of the door, the polygonal window, the upended pillars or 'estípites', and larger and smaller niches, is blurred by the infinite foam-like sparkle of the decoration, but not wholly lost. Its general distribution and individual details such as consoles, medallions and canopies, conspire to make the church façade into a retable rising with slim brilliance into the translucent sky.

The church consists of a single nave and is built in the form of a Latin cross. Beneath the accumulation of paintings, and even more retables, it is transformed into a kind of marine palace bathed on all sides in a transparent, golden light. Painted decoration, often of high quality, appears here and there, but the walls are far more forcefully enveloped by the gold of the retables; their lavish woodcarvings cover the surroundings of the high altar and transept, and come to life in the light of the dome. The richly adorned volumes of the church are remarkable as the simple boundaries assigned to them by walls and vaults disappear. Other limits are substituted for them: a vague borderline of subdued paintings and gilded wood which shimmer before our eyes.

On the left, the chapel of St Joseph and the repro-

duction of the Casa de Loreto also owe their beauty to the richness of the decoration covering their sharply defined volumes; it reaches an unusual degree of density in the octagonal 'camarín' at the rear where pilasters with silver figures, 'azulejos' lining the lower walls, statues of archangels, and ribs similar to those of the mosque at Cordova, combine to form an enclosed world in which religious faith is heightened by colour and elegance.

Tlaxcala (Mexico): Sanctuary of Ocotlán

Even after a lengthy visit, which deepens one's knowledge of the building, the sanctuary of the Virgin of Ocotlán calls to mind a succession of vignettes all relating to the façade of the church. This façade is white round the door and in its central portion, termed by Mexicans the 'imafronte'. The bell towers are also white, except for their narrow bases, which are pink bordering on red, the colour of the flat set bricks.

The church stands on an eminence facing a mountainous horizon, a short distance from Tlaxcala. The façade rises upward, as we have just said, in an almost obsessive way; it can be seen above the inward curving walls which form the boundary of the square or atrium and between the grilles of the gates, framed by pilasters of gleaming white, rivalling that of the towers. It reveals itself in close-up from the actual atrium, from where one may take in the entire interplay of colours and shapes.

The pure white central section is sheltered beneath a great arch resembling with its fluting the rim of a sea shell; it consists of two storeys with 'estípites' arranged round the door and a clerestory window. In front of this window stands a statue of the Virgin shielded by the curtains of a baldacchino. Angels unfurl their wings at regular intervals. The space outlined by the bases of the towers and the great fluted arch cannot be defined; it opens up a world of spiritual and aesthetic values. Contemplation of the twin bell towers offers a fresh source of inspiration, for they repeat both the colour and the motifs of the central section, and seem to soar up into the sky with greater intensity as they are set on narrower bases.

The usual tendencies may be found within. The simple architectural volumes – a single nave of three bays, a dome forward of the high altar, and its surroundings – are set off by the brilliance of the retables which help one to ignore the mediocrity of the paintings in the nave.

The 'camarín' behind has a surprise in store. Built to an octagonal plan, lit by a line of curvilinear attic windows, and totally covered with sculptures, it forms a casket dedicated to the glory of the Virgin and arranged round the dove of the Holy Spirit placed in the centre of the dome. This is not the place to speak of the horror of the void associated with mudéjar architecture. Equally, the terms 'riot of ornament' and 'vertigo of the spectator' are insufficient in this context because they merely concern aesthetics and have little or no religious connotation. Those who commissioned and realized this masterpiece did so with the aim of evoking religious emotion; joy in art, which is our aim, constitutes a profane and unexpected reaction.

Taxco (Mexico): Santa Prisca

Although we are still within the borders of the same catholic and artistic world at Santa Prisca, we shall not find either the rich complexity of Tepotzotlán or the highly coloured lyricism of Ocotlán. Here the upward surge of the building accords with its vigorous stylistic unity and the extremely clear articulation of its spaces and volumes. The visitor can guess the history of the building: the will of one man governed the entire enterprise and imposed on it its exact design.

The composition of Santa Prisca is perfectly clear. It is set in the heart of a landscape of wooded mountains surrounding the little town, the two towers of the façade frame the 'imafronte' and, behind, the dome rises above the transept. Within, the clearly defined volumes of the Latin cross plan are echoed by others just as clear, – the sacristy behind the high altar, the chapel of the Indians, and various subsidiary divisions on either side of the nave.

Yet this clarity, which seems so interesting to a practised eye, is not wholly obvious, The main emphasis comes from decoration richly spread over the 'imafronte' and the bell towers but does not extend to the bases of the towers in accordance with the principle already noted at Ocotlán. It adorns the wavy cornice of the nave walls and is discreetly used on the envelope of the dome. In this way the exterior contours of the church are endowed with an airy vagueness, whilst the interior decoration softens the hardness of the volumes which might otherwise appear over-simple. As in the churches we have already visited, though in a very homogeneous style, the retables glow and the stone has been lavishly carved; here and there paintings fill portions of the walls and altars. These various features make for ill-defined boundaries that cause the vaults of the building to recede, substituting for them a new, subtle, almost hazy composition.

Thus the three Mexican buildings we have just examined add substantially to our vision of the Hispanic-type church. Now let us try to define that vision.

A singular animation emanates from these buildings, largely attributable to the two towers of the main façade and the dome set back, usually above the transept crossing; it is also due to the abundance of ornament which deprives lines and masses of too rigid an appearance. The architects seem to have voluntarily foregone a purely geometrical approach, and endeavoured to envelop their buildings in a network of ornament. Nevertheless, the simplicity of the composition is plainly evident to the practised eye. It produces an effect of lightness: the towers above the often single naves are set against the sky with a remarkable mixture of strength and fragility, creating a skyline in which the dome constitutes both an architectural theme, its mass contrasting happily with that of the towers, and a landmark in the infinity of the sky. Set against the lyrical light of the sky the silhouettes of these Hispanic baroque churches with their blurred outlines seem to be variants on extremely simple traditional plans.

Analysis of the interiors takes time. From the moment he enters the visitor is overcome by the richness of the decoration which envelops him on all sides, a dream-world of ornament, sumptuous through its materials, colour and diversity. The varied resources of the Hispanic genius have contributed to the success of the general effect. Ceramic facings, 'azulejos', sometimes cover the lower sections of the walls. Retables rise from the altars to the vaults and the gilded woods from which they are carved often extend from their individual spheres; sometimes their richness overflows to link up with the frames of their neighbours. Paintings, both frescoes and on canvas, cover wide areas of the walls, sections of the vaults, the pendentives of the dome and the dome itself, whilst lively motifs in plaster and stucco spread sometimes over the entire church, sometimes over part of it. The technique of sculptured stone creates a more restrained atmosphere of beauty, displaying its elegance on pillars and columns or in the upper areas of the structure.

The interiors of these churches are, nevertheless, made up of clearly defined volumes, built to a simple plan and juxtaposed almost at random. They are like interlocking stone boxes over which the magnificence of the decoration flows freely.

Thus decoration is of prime importance. On exteriors it is specially abundant round doors and windows, expanding over shields and bas-reliefs. As may be seen at a glance, it is not only diffuse but luxuriant and light. It is often restricted to the upper sections as if the ornamental vegetation could freely expand when released from the weight of the building.

This is the pattern of the Hispanic type church throughout Spain and her former American possessions. To these characteristics must be added the achievement of two enclosed spaces which the visitor cannot ignore: the 'sagrario' where the Holy Sacrament is kept and worshipped, and the 'camarín', whose intimate, withdrawn beauty suggests a casket of precious stones.

To these common features the various regions of Spain and America add their own individual touches.

Ecija: Palace of the Marquises of Peñaflor

The visitor who walks through Ecija, a typical Andalusian town, some of its white houses covered with flowers, will not suddenly come upon a free standing palace. Instead, he will find in the Calle Caballeros, a narrow street wafting memories of lost elegance, a concave façade notable for its length and its wrought iron balcony, supported by iron brackets, which lends it a sense of continuity. This façade is all the more surprising because of the unexpected splendour of the upper storey, where the real windows are set in 'trompe-l'œil' architecture. At one end of this concave wall with its elegant, untiring sense of movement, rises the main doorway, emphasised by pairs of columns rising over two storeys, a profusion of sculpture, and bold coping.

The patio is white, light, scented, and filled with music – the murmuring water in the central fountain resembles the singing of a pair of happy birds. The detail of the architecture may well be overlooked with all these seductive charms, – two galleries, open arcades at ground level, the upper one enclosed, with windows beneath the arches.

Façade, main doorway and patio surprise and charm. The staircase is singularly impressive. The cage through which it rises is reached by three open arches at ground level; it has ingenious spatial divisions and is elegantly and imaginatively decorated with plaster motifs surrounding the various sections and framing a painting dedicated to the Virgin; finally, it expands beneath a dome. The dignity of the composition, the elegant perspectives viewed throughout the ascent, and the richness of the decorations all help to create a masterpiece.

Antigua (Guatemala): University

The magnificence of the buildings of Spain, Mexico and Peru most frequently strikes the traveller. Yet here is another characteristic which may detain and captivate him, – lyrical grace. This seems typical of the architecture of Central America, if one may judge from the buildings of Antigua. This city, under its original name of Santiago de los Caballeros de Guatemala, was the capital of a vast region, extending from what is now Chiapas in Southern Mexico to the frontiers of Panama. Earthquakes here are a natural and inevitable scourge, more so perhaps than in any other part of Spanish America, and that of St Martha's day, 1773, led to the abandonment of the city and the foundation of the present capital. Santiago de los Caballeros, now Antigua, still maintains a sizeable population but, with some of its buildings still in ruins, looks like a baroque version of Pompeii; the volcanoes of Agua, Fuego and Acatenango have never buried it completely, but there is a continual threat that they might.

There should be a dramatic atmosphere in the heart of this city smitten by death and destruction, where the buildings have been only partially restored and another earthquake is a constant possibility; it is not melancholy, however, because the poetry of the ruins and the gentleness of nature endow it with an extraordinary softness. The University stands near the cathedral and the palace of the captains-general, portions of which survive or else have been repaired. It can be found quite easily thanks to the checkerboard plan usually adopted in American cities. The building seems fairly low (it consists of ground-floor only), but is blindingly white. Papal crests, polygonal windows set high up, and brackets in low relief stress the recession of the walls. The most beautiful feature is within the building: a patio, just as dazzling as the exterior, but lightened by the subtle inflections of the arches and kept fresh by the tinkling fountain in the centre. We are made to forget that the materials used are relatively poor and that sturdy pillars replace columns as supports for the galleries. The charm of the place grips the heart, whilst the eye notes how cleverly the striated surfaces, the cushions of the consoles, and the inverted S's alleviate the weight of the structure.

As has already been noted at Ecija, the palaces of the period place great emphasis on their staircases. Both palaces and universities arrange their plans and decorative schemes round their patios, which are made the object of special attention as centres for private and scholastic life. In general, the decoration of secular buildings, like religious, is spread over a relatively simple structure.

Perhaps the buildings of Portugal and Brazil will suggest similar conclusions.

Ouro Preto (Brazil): São Francisco

The church of the Third Order of St Francis at Ouro Preto in the province of Minas Geraes, a district recalling the prosperity of its mining period, resembles a jewel in a casket.

The casket is the airy oval on which the building stands. By its position the monastery appears as vast as the sky. The jewel is the actual façade: white panels inserted amid carved stone, the flanking towers perceptibly recessed to give the building a partially convex design, the central section with magnificent sculptures within the door frame and a medallion portraying the ecstasy of St Francis.

The simple elegance of this façade renders it almost fragile and gives it complete unity of composition. On the other hand, the wide spreading sides of the church do not aim at beauty, nor do they appear to express any particular aesthetic. The entire building forms a compact, elongated block. Its façade and towers, endowed with a variety of undulating movement, are its most charming features.

The seductive yet compact nature of the building is confirmed by the interior. Carved wood and paintings envelop the elongated, occasionally constricted volumes in a warm atmosphere of joyfulness and

Venezuela

British Guiana

Dutch Guiana

French Guiana

Colombia

Ecuador

Peru

Brazil

Lake Titicaca

La Paz

Pomata

Bolivia

Minas Geraes

Congonhas
do Campo

Ouro Preto

Rio de Janeiro

Paraguay

Chile

Argentina

Uruguay

1 Caracas
2 Bogota
3 Cali
4 Quito
5 Lima
6 Cuzco
7 Arequipa
8 Puno
9 Potosi
10 Santiago du Chile
11 Córdoba
12 Buenos Aires
13 São Paulo
14 Sabará
15 Bahia
16 Recife

Map of Latin America

colour. The practised eye will note stylistic differences between the high altar, with its subtly curved lines and motifs, and the side altars and paintings which, in the nave vaults, are dedicated to the Immaculate Conception. These differences do not, however, affect the magic lightness and gaiety of the composition. A more important discovery is reserved for anyone penetrating further to the back of the church. In the rear half of the building, to the sides of and behind the high altar, is a succession of corridors and ancillary spaces designed not merely as appendices to the building but as divisions within a compact plan.

So far as São Francisco allows us to generalize for the Luso-Brazilian world, interior decoration tends to be a substitute for structure, thus creating indeterminate boundaries – a characteristic shared by the buildings we have already visited in Spain and Spanish America. On the other hand, the compact plan inherited by Brazil from Portugal is unmistakeably an original feature of Hispanic architecture.

Braga: Bom Jesus do Monte

The difference in spirit is just as noticeable in an undertaking connected not only with architecture in the strict sense of the word but with the layout of an entire site – buildings, gardens and landscape. This is the sanctuary of the Bom Jesus near Braga.

As soon as one enters the complex, one feels the special quality of the atmosphere. It combines a typically Portuguese feeling for elegance with the picturesqueness of nature arranged in accordance with an exact design, the several stages of a pilgrimage, and iconographic symbolism.

It is set in the serene, softly coloured, homely region of the Minho. Beyond the entrance portico and its two fountains we have to scale the winding road, bordered by chapels, which forms the Via Sacra of the pilgrimage. After a landing, when the fountain of the Five Wounds of Christ resembles a huge surprising plant with its exuberant vegetable decora-

tion, we mount the staircases of the Five Senses and of the Theological Virtues and arrive at the church.

Suzanne Chantal and José Augusto dos Santos have aptly described this itinerary and analysed its atmosphere. 'The Bom Jesus at the top of its monumental staircase scaling the lofty hill of Monte Espinho, receives pilgrims all the year round. The Via Sacra first winds between thick clumps of trees studded with chapels containing the fourteen Stations of the Cross bathed in a theatrical light. Finally we arrive at a dignified double staircase which opens and closes like a fan; it is divided by landings ornamented with curious statues – the Five Senses followed by the Virtues – and leads to an upper terrace watched over by helmeted horsemen and edged by stone balustrades.'

The two authors also subtly define the visitor's varying emotions, which match the changes in the landscape. 'For the walker, the ascent to the Bom Jesus is a slow stroll in the park of some eccentric prince; he is bathed in an unsettling form of lyricism springing from the harmonious contrast between lush, perfumed gardens and the stone of the statues whose rich baroque shapes bristling with plumes and tassels are outlined against the bright blue sky. The slope is so steep that the huge, shady esplanade by the sanctuary, crowded with sellers of medals and statues and tables serving lemonade and confectionery, is not disclosed until the last step.'

This layout is more than a spatial creation; with its carefully prepared perspectives and routes, it is a self-contained microcosm opening on to a magnificent landscape. 'The Bom Jesus at Braga offers everyone, whether pious pilgrims or ordinary walkers, freshness and light, gardens perfumed with eucalyptus and Spanish broom, and a wide panorama embracing the countless belfries of Braga...'

Such is the architecture of our sphere of study seen in the light of several characteristic buildings. Now we must find an answer to the basic question: does this architecture derive from baroque art?

Plates

Saragossa

57 Cathedral of the Pilar, façade to the Ebro. The building is set between the river and a vast square and so offers two main façades. The composition is easily read: axes for circulation separate the outer chapels from the central section of the building housing the 'capilla mayor', the 'coro' and the Chapel of the Pilar.

58 The central dome combines overtones of the dome of St Peter's, Rome, with a Hispanic flavour.

59 Interior of the central dome; the elegance of the design respects the divisions imposed by the structure.

60 Portico leading to Chapel of the Pilar. This chapel forms an independent building within the cathedral.

61 Detail showing part of the structure of the cathedral (dome) above the portico of the Chapel of the Pilar.

Salamanca

62 Clerecía (former Jesuit College), general view. The scale of the building is impressive and there is a striking contrast between the lavishly decorated upper portions of the church and the austere yet lively geometry of the College building.

63 Façade of the church, central section. The richness of the decoration increases with the height. The bell towers and the gable belong to the florid type of Baroque.

64 The dignified and sumptuous cloister is contemporary with the bell towers.

65 Detail of the cloister. The column in the centre makes a powerful upward thrust; decoration runs riot over the capital and within the arches to either side.

66 Interior of the dome of the church. The decoration springs from the sculptured stone.

67 Cloister gallery. The austerity is only mitigated by the double arches and pilasters and the linear decoration.

Seville

68 San Luis, church of the former Novitiate of the Jesuits. By its decoration the façade registers a 'horror of the void' (statues, striated surfaces, columns and pilasters wreathed with ornament).

69 Interior of the dome. The church is built to a circular plan and the dome prolongs the central space by a concentric, upward movement.

70 Dome and apse above the entrance. Four semicircular chapels in the form of apses or niches radiate from the central space.

71 Altar of St Francis-Xavier between two of the semicircular chapels.

72 Detail of the dome and of the niche above the altar of St Stanislas Kotska.

73 Right: altar of St Stanislas Kotska with the saint's statue by Pedro Duque Cornejo; left: stoup in the private chapel of the Novitiate.

Tepotzotlán (Former Jesuit College, now Museum of the Viceroyalty)

74 Façade of the church, mid-height. This detail illustrates the monumental rhythm set in motion by the 'estípites', the polygonal rose-window and the niches.

75 Detail of the façade: statue of a bishop.

76 Church, main altar, dedicated to St Francis-Xavier.

77 Church, altar of Our Lady of Light (1758).

78 Church, detail of upper portions of transept.

79 Private chapel, altar (restored in 1950).

80 Dome of the 'camarín', behind the Santa Casa de Loreto. The outline of the arches is reminiscent of the mosque at Cordova, recalling the importance of the 'mudéjar' tradition in Spanish America. In the lantern the dove of the Holy Spirit descends upon the Virgin and Apostles.

Clerecía, Salamanca (Church and College of the Jesuits)
Plan 1:1000 and section 1:333

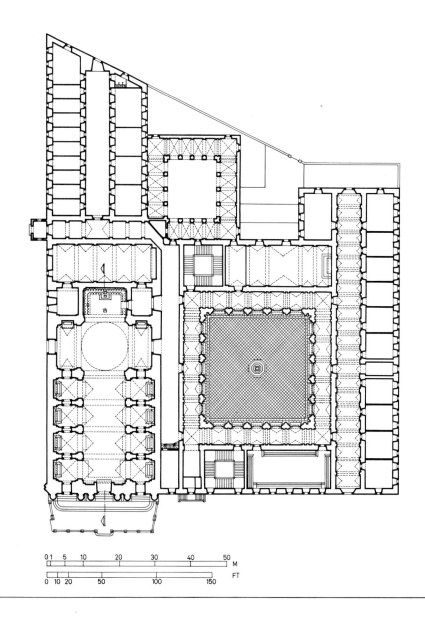

0 1 5 10   20   30   40   50
                                              M

0 10 20   50   100   150   FT

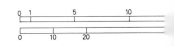

0 1   5   10

0   10   20

Notes

Saragossa

Cathedral of the Pilar. According to revered tradition, the Virgin appeared to St James the Great in the year 40 to encourage him to preach the Gospel throughout the Spanish peninsular. The pillar of this apparition became an object of special veneration and a chapel was erected on the site. A later building constructed after the Reconquest was burnt in 1434, restored, and then replaced after 1515 by a Gothic church. The devotion of the Spaniards to the Virgin of the Pilar explains why the structure dedicated to the apparition was made a cathedral equal to the Seo in 1675, and caused the decision to erect a new building in 1677. The design of Felipe Sánchez which included corner towers was modified by Herrera the Younger in 1660; he was responsible for the idea of twin façades facing the plaza and the Ebro and for circulatory aisles surrounding a central space destined for services and the chapel of the apparition. Later changes resulted in the reestablishment of corner towers and a multiplicity of domes. Ventura Rodríguez designed the chapel of the apparition combining ingenuity with a sense of grandeur (1751). Francisco and Ramón Bayeu, Goya and González Velázquez worked on frescoes for the cathedral during the second half of the 18th century.

Salamanca

Clerecía. This royal college in the charge of the Jesuits was founded in 1614. The original plans are by Juan Gómez de Mora who devised a large, U-shaped edifice comprising a church and seven-storey buildings; the composition seems to impose both its mass of stone and its moral guardianship upon the city. The somewhat functional regularity of the college building makes a majestic effect and the façades justify Kubler's epithet of 'a precocious dynamism of surfaces'. The interior of the church has a rich, regal clarity and also reveals the talent of Juan Gómez de Mora. Nevertheless, the completion of the Clerecía in the mid-18th century has resulted in certain sections being endowed with different characteristics. The bell towers of the façade and the grandiose patio (1750–1755) are, in fact, the work of Andrés García de Quiñones. In its bold lyricism the patio recalls both Roman and German architecture and, through the latter, is related to certain details at Mafra.

Seville

San Luis. This church of the Jesuit novitiate, placed under the patronage of St Louis of France, has been attributed by Antonio Sancho Corbacho to Luis de Figueroa. Work on the foundations started on April 14, 1699 and the solemn consecration of the church took place in 1731, one year after the architect's death. On account of its rich decoration the church has been called 'the most representative building of the first manifestation of 18th century Baroque' in the region of Seville; this richness is expressed in the abundance and variety of the exterior ornament and the lavish materials used in the interior. The sculptures are the work of Pedro Duque Cornejo, Juan de Hinestrosa and their assistants, and the paintings are by Domingo Martínez and Lucas Valdés (1743). The actual architecture bears some resemblances to Italian Renaissance and Baroque. The lower section of the façade and the circular plan are similar to Sant' Agnese in Piazza Navona in Rome. Indeed, this type of plan was used by Michelangelo for St Peter's and by Palladio at the Villa Rotonda near Vicenza; it was also used by Carlo Fontana for the church of the Jesuit sanctuary of Loyola (1681). The private chapel slightly to the rear of the church was built to a rectangular plan. Polychrome plaster medallions and sculptured wood play a large part in the decoration.

Tepotzotlán

The colleges of Tepotzotlán formed one of the most important Jesuit establishments not only in Mexico but in the whole of the New World. In obedience to the summons of the Archbishop of Mexico about 1580, the Fathers founded a college destined exclusively for Indian children, under the patronage of St Martin; to this they later added a novitiate. The whole complex of buildings set around several patios belonged to the Jesuits until they were expelled by Charles III in 1767. The church of St Francis-Xavier and its ancillary buildings represent a century of Mexican Baroque; the actual church was built in twelve years (May 25, 1670–September 9, 1682), the Casa de Loreto and its 'camarín' were inaugurated on December 25, 1733, and the chapel of St Joseph on April 27, 1738. The retables of the church date from 1755–1758 and the façade, by an unknown architect, from 1760–1762. The private chapel was built in the second half of the 17th century and decorated about the middle of the 18th century. Tepotzotlán has been restored and since 1964 has been used as the Museum of the Viceroyalty.

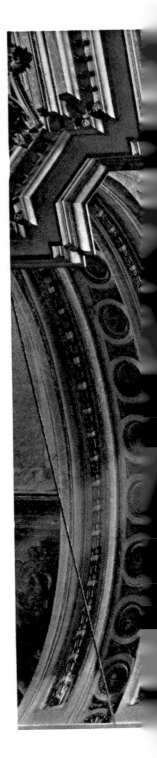

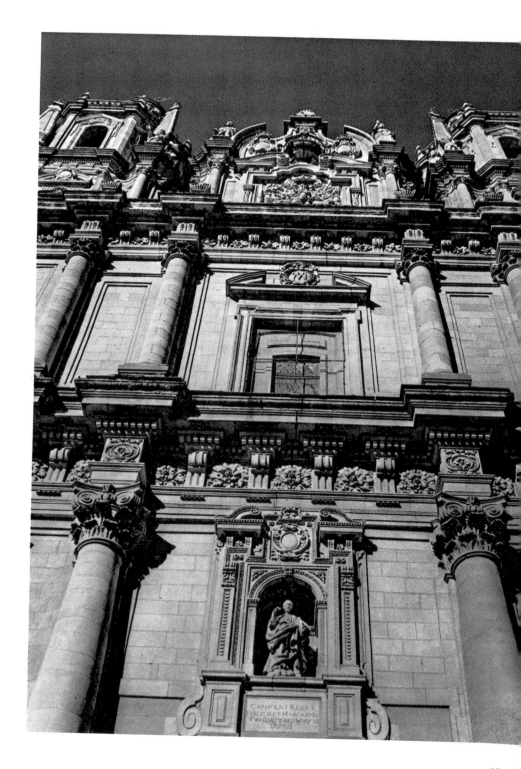

65

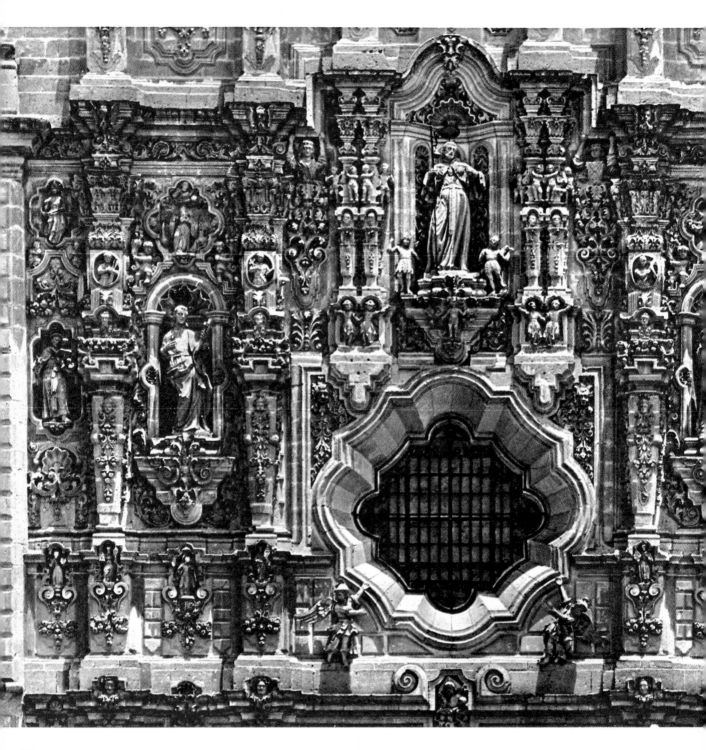

Church of San Luis, Seville
Section and plans 1:500

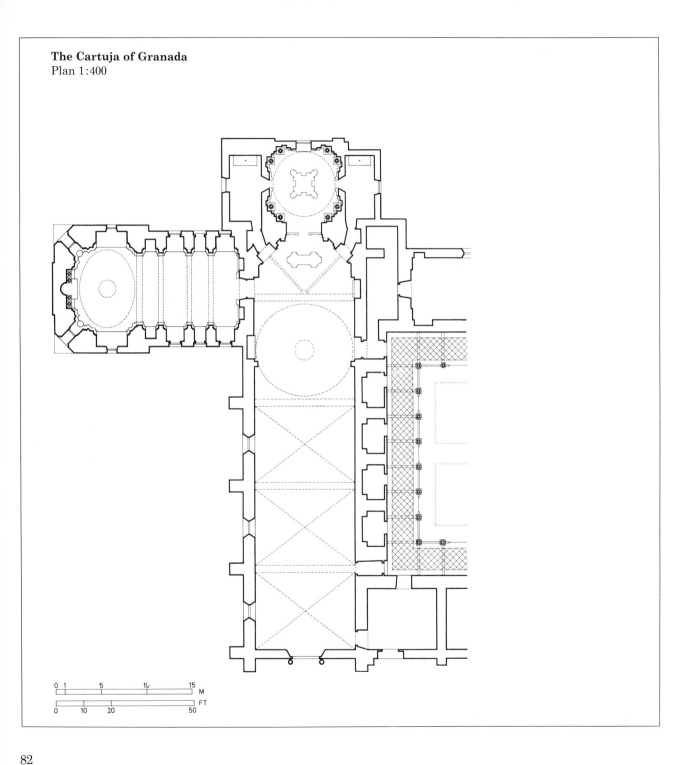

The Cartuja of Granada
Plan 1:400

0 1   5   10   15
                      M
0   10   20   50
                  FT

3. Style and architectural conception

An attempt to define baroque architecture

Defining baroque architecture is a difficult undertaking. As far as the Iberian peninsular is concerned, it might seem natural to look for it in the pages of Eugenio d'Ors, the inspired interpreter of 'forms which take flight'; his thoughts and writings, however, were those of a seer rather than of a historian bound to exact definitions. Heinrich Wölfflin in his 'Principles of art history' worked out five types of contradiction between Renaissance and Baroque which are only obvious in extreme cases.

The Renaissance is linear, the Baroque pictorial: 'In the former, accentuation is on the boundaries of objects, in the latter one's vision runs beyond exact limits'. Baroque is 'the flux of changing perspectives' and 'its forms must be able to breathe'. Renaissance architecture is revealed in plane surfaces, Baroque in depth. The former indicates closed, fixed, serene forms, the latter open, tense, dynamic, fluid forms moving on to dissolution. The Renaissance is unified, the Baroque multiform. The Renaissance is absolute clarity, the Baroque relative clarity focussed on the objects presented. In 1913 Jean Rousset gave a clear, concise definition that defies argument. Baroque architecture consists of 'the interpretation of forms embedded in dynamic compositions unified and animated by expanding movement. The effect produced on the spectator is a mixture of instability and theatrical illusion'.

To his definition may be added Philippe Minguet's analysis of 1966. To some extent this seems contradictory, but it rightly insists on the impossibility of 'forcibly reducing the baroque style to one basic characteristic'. Turning to architecture it spotlights 'the lack of balance in construction, the separation of structure from ornament, the break-up of unity, the hints of the dynamic, and the tendency to indulge in the colossal for the sake of sheer effect'.

Bearing in mind the impossibility deprecated by Minguet, we may consider baroque architecture as displaying most, if not all, of the following features – a desire for the grandiose, a tendency to illusionary effects, richness of decoration, and a dynamic approach to plan and space.

Baroque architecture and Spanish temperament

Although economic conditions and collective psychology in Spain and her American dominions were favourable to the Baroque, the permanent architectural features expressive of the national temperament were only in partial agreement with the tendencies enumerated above.

Spain had experienced the alternation of austere and richly decorated styles of architecture to a more contrasted degree than most other countries. The richness of decoration was due to the interplay of the people's basic inclinations and the strength of the influences to which they had been subjected since

Cárcel de Corte, or prison, Madrid. Now the Ministry of Foreign Affairs: façade by Juan Gomez de Mora, 1629 (after Kubler and Soria)

the foundation of Hispanic civilization – Moorish and Mudéjar art followed by Flemish and Germanic. The classic Renaissance style imported from Italy only concerned a restricted circle around Charles V and Philip II. Decoration was diffuse and flat with a regular repetition of similar motifs, arranged within rectangular frames applied to the walls of buildings. Late 15th and early 16th century façades were conceived as huge altar pieces similar to those which stretched from floor to vault inside the churches. A pre-established harmony existed between this tradition and the dynamic decoration of the Baroque.

On the other hand, there was a basic opposition in plan and mass. The French and Italian conception of architectural space was a void contained within walls. The Spaniards, however, preferred to divide it up in a manner closer to nature, possibly because of the mountains which partitioned their country, or, more probably, because the Church favoured an individual conception of worship.

The Spaniards imported their conception of architecture into America. It was already in harmony with two characteristics of the Indian temperament: the

Valladolid Cathedral, by Juan de Herrera, 1585: plan (after O. Schubert)

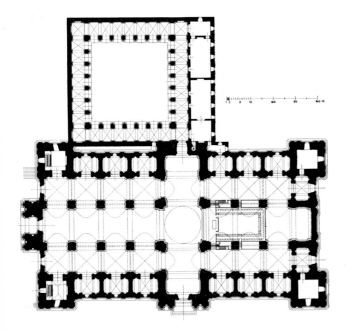

lavishness of thickly applied, relatively flat decoration, and the construction of vast buildings as practised by the Mayas, with an accumulation of small units rather than large-scale rooms. The first aspect favoured the Baroque, but not the second, as it resulted in architectural division. On the other hand, the desire to impress the Indians with sumptuous churches declaring the superiority of the Christian religion, and the opportunity of building them on wide spaces set in the heart of the new towns, were bound to accentuate the monumental and theatrical characteristics of the architecture.

This heralded a decorative rather then a structural type of Baroque, stressed by the contrast between the simple building materials which included stone, limestone, Galician granite, Andalusian brick, and tezontle, a volcanic stone from Mexico, and the rich, varied materials used for the ornamentation.

Evolution of style in Spain: the respective roles of structure and decoration

Generally the baroque feeling for plan and mass revealed itself late in Spain; these remained static in the traditional manner, whereas façade and interior ornament tended to run riot in an excess of movement.

Until about 1680, at any rate in the north in Castile and Galicia, the dominant influence in architecture was Juan de Herrera, whose most important works include the palace-monastery of the Escorial and the unfinished cathedral at Valladolid; now, however, his style was embodied in a new form. Up till 1610 or so and occasionally later, a picturesque surface effect was obtained by a flexible use of shapes and chiaroscuro which seemed to cover façades in a wicker network. This tendency could already be noted in the work of Francisco de Mora who built the town of Lerma for the Duke of Lerma, favourite of Philip III (1605), and it was even more prominent from about 1610 to 1640 in that of his nephew Juan Gómez de Mora who began the Clerecía at Salamanca in 1614 and designed the Plaza Mayor (1617–19) and prob-

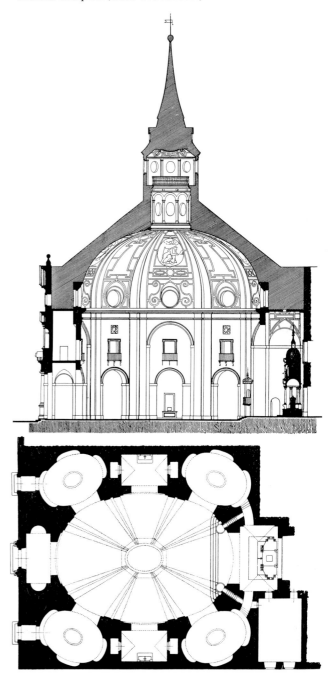

Bernadas Church, Alcalá de Henares, by J.G. de Mora: section and plan (after O. Schubert)

ably the Cárcel de Corte at Madrid in 1629–35; to use a happy phrase of George Kubler it turned into 'a precocious surface dynamism'. A similar development may be noted at the palace of Buen Retiro (1631–33) and the Dominican church of Loeches (1635–38) near Madrid by Alonso Carbonell who made skilful use of geometrical compartments as surface divisions. The sole example of Juan de Herrera's work in Andalusia was the Lonja at Seville, but, having adopted Italian Mannerism and continuing to assimilate it, the province contributed to the general movement with coffered stucco decorations in churches, and façades divided by panels and pilasters; one of the most attractive examples of this style is the Sagrario of Seville cathedral by Juan de Zumárraga (1617). The Baroque typified by curved plans and spatial complexity makes no appearance except in Sebastián de la Plaza's oval Bernardas Chapel (1617–26) at Alcalá de Henares, which derives from Serlio. The churches built by the Jesuit Bautista for his order from 1628 onwards – San Juan Bautista at Toledo and San Isidro at Madrid – are directly influenced by the Roman architecture of Giacomo della Porta.

The years 1600–40 merely form an introduction to the general development, but special attention should be paid to them, for they clearly indicate how 17th and 18th century Spain almost always created her own picturesque style; this later became more and more overloaded not so much from plans and decoration borrowed from contemporary Italy as from the individual transformation of earlier Italian motifs.

This tendency was confirmed over the period 1640 to 1680 which witnessed the first experiments whose successful results continued up till the arrival of Neo-Classicism. There was a vast increase in the great ceremonies which were the delight of the baroque age – secular and religious festivals and funerary pomp. Sebastián de Herrera Barnuevo's catafalque for Philip IV (1665) in the Encarnación at Madrid with its resemblance to a canopied retable, and the 'triunfo' designed by Bernardo Simón de Pineda for the cannonization of St Ferdinand in Seville Cathedral, with

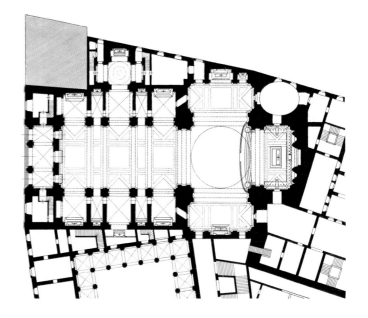

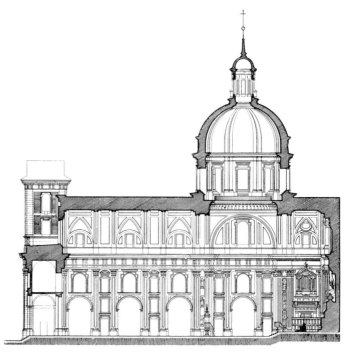

Church of San Isidro el Real, Madrid: plan and longitudinal section (after O. Schubert)

86

its jagged decoration, are basic stages in this stylistic development. The churches were filled with theatrical retables such as the one devised by Pineda as a frame for the Burial of Christ by Pedro Roldán (1670) in the chapel of the Caridad in Seville. Façades, too, began to resemble retables as in the case of the tower of San Miguel at Jerez (after 1672) by Diego Moreno Meléndez, whose crowded decoration is reminiscent of Mexico and that at the entrance to the Cartuja outside the town (1667).

The pattern of the 'camarín', devised for the worship of relics or statues and set in twin relationship to the church it served, was established in the Chapel of San Isidro, San Andrés, Madrid, by Pedro de la Torre (after 1642) and at the Virgen de los Desamparados, Valencia, by Diego Martínez Ponce de Urrana (1647–67).

Despite his stay in Italy, Francisco de Herrera the younger was not influenced by Italian Baroque in the plan he presented for the cathedral of the Pilar at Saragossa in 1680. Nor did José Ximénez Donoso, after living for several years in Rome (1647–54), bring back home any hint of the contemporary architecture which he had been able to study there. When Velázquez was commissioned to renovate the Alcázar

at Madrid, he made brilliant use of Italian baroque decoration in the octagonal saloon (1657) and in the hall of mirrors (1659), but this successful treatment was limited to court art and its sphere of influence.

Guarino Guarini, the designer of Santa Maria Divina Providéncia at Lisbon, probably crossed Spain in 1666–68, but, far from introducing his subtle form of Baroque there, he imbibed the idea of ribbed vaults in the mudéjar tradition. Carlo Fontana's plan of 1681 for the great Jesuit monastery at Loyola arranged an impressive group of courtyards and buildings round the sides and back of the circular chapel; but construction was slow and took on Spanish characteristics. Giovanni Battista Contini, another of Bernini's pupils, designed the tower of the Seo, the old cathedral of Saragossa in 1683; this was faithfully carried out by local architects, but was still unfinished when the Abbé Ponz, author of the 'Viaje de España', published his description of the city in 1788. Such limited connections, revealing the weak influence of Italian Baroque, contrast with the brilliance and local spread of the design of some Spanish buildings such as the 'envelope' erected round the Romanesque cathedral at Compostela, in particular the Campanas and Reloj towers by José Peña de Toro (died 1676) and Domingo de Andrade (c. 1639–1712).

José Benito de Churriguera (1665–1725), who was the eldest of five brothers all architects and decorators like himself, revealed himself at Madrid and Salamanca as a very different artist from the traditional image accorded to him. He did not personify the style of his period, so this cannot be generally termed Churrigueresque. He was much more than a mere sculptor of retables, a conservative artist more or less at a loss in building construction. At Nuevo Baztán he appears in the threefold guise of town planner, architect, and sculptor, recalling Juan de Herrera in his handling of masses and linking this with richness of decoration. In the three sacristies of the Cartuja (1702–20) and the cathedral (after 1704) at Granada, and of the Cartuja at Paular near Segovia (after 1718), Francisco Hurtado (1669–1725) showed himself a geometrician and expert in a luminous,

Chapel of San Isidro, San Andrés, Madrid: plan (after O. Schubert)

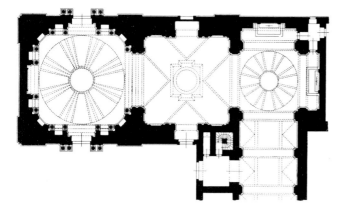

highly coloured form of art, heralding the following period in Andalusia. Leonardo de Figueroa (c. 1650 to 1730) spent his prolific working life at Seville where he produced his masterpiece, the church of San Telmo, after 1724; the general appearance of the façade resembles the Lonja, but the main door is a rare successful example of lyrical balance.

From about 1720 to 1770 building construction tended to be outweighed by decoration, and ornament was inclined to disintegrate. This period ended with the triumph of Neo-Classicism, which benefited from Charles III's decision in 1777 to submit all public works to examination by the Academia de San Fernando and from his recommendation to the clergy to do the same. The Solomonic column gave way to the 'estípite', a type of upturned pyramid, somewhat distorted.

This was the period of the 'delirious fools', the 'fatuos delirantes', as they were branded by Llaguno. In actual fact, highly talented architects came to the fore in each of the great cities of Spain. In Madrid, Pedro de Ribera (c. 1683–1742) designed the Toledo Bridge (1719–24) and the Hospice of San Fernando (after 1722). At Valladolid the Tomé family was responsible for the University façade (1715) and at Toledo, Narciso, the most famous member of this family, completed the Transparente in the cathedral (1721–32). In Salamanca, Alberto de Churriguera (1676–1750) began the Plaza Mayor (after 1728), which was finished by Andrés García de Quiñones, the builder of the towers and cloister of the Clerecía (1750–55). Finally, at Compostela, Fernando de Casas y Novoa began the Obradoiro of the cathedral in 1738; this was completed shortly after his death in 1749.

The growing importance and occasional disintegration of decoration were merely two facets of Spanish architecture during the twofold period 1680–1770. Other characteristics derived from foreign influences – either Italian Baroque, or the Rococo of monarchical France. The Mediterranean provinces were always particularly susceptible to the former and this tradition gained added impetus in 1708–11 from the presence of Ferdinando Galli-Bibiena in Barcelona at the court of the Archduke Charles, pretender to the Spanish throne. From 1700 onwards the new Bourbon dynasty reigned in Madrid and imposed the French monarchical pattern, though at the same time showing a marked sympathy towards the Italian style.

This style may be noted between 1699 and 1731 in San Luis, the church of the novitiate of the Jesuits at Seville, attributed to Leonardo de Figueroa; this is a circular central plan building with the lower storey corresponding to the design of Sant' Agnese in the Piazza Navona in Rome. At Valencia, between 1701 and 1707, Conrad Rudolf, a German by birth trained in Paris and subsequently in Rome, produced a design for the door of the cathedral whose concave and convex lines take their inspiration from Bernini's first project for the east front of the Louvre and from Guarini's church of San Lorenzo in Turin. At Murcia, Jaime Bort conceived the façade of the cathedral as a spirited interplay of lines and plane surfaces centred on a great inward curving porch (1735–49). In the façade of the cathedral of Guadix, Vicente Acero y Arebo combined plateresque themes with the concave curves of the buttresses (1714–20). Pedro de Ribera also made use of baroque silhouettes and proportions in the church of the Virgen del Puerto (1718) and in his design for the Royal Palace at Madrid (1735).

These buildings are related to baroque architecture through their plans and proportions, but it remains a Hispanic Baroque. Court art, on the other hand, introduced an international Baroque in which barely modified Italian sources prevailed. At La Granja, the favourite residence of Philip V, the original palace (1721–23), conceived by Ardemáns as an Alcázar, was remodelled by Procaccini, Juvara and Sacchetti (completed 1741). These sources also explain the Royal Palace at Madrid built by Sacchetti, who adapted a project by Juvara (1735–64), Bonavia's church of San Miguel at Madrid (1735) with its graceful convex façade, and his chapel of San Antonio in Aranjuez, and San Marcos in Madrid by Ventura Rodríguez (1749–53).

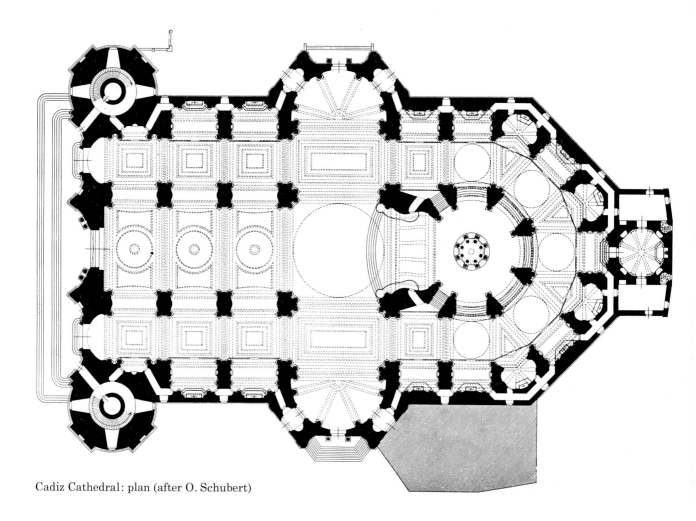

Cadiz Cathedral: plan (after O. Schubert)

Because Rodríguez worked with Juvara and Sacchetti, he was able to bring about a synthesis between Hispanic and international Baroque without ever having been to Italy. Unfortunately, on Charles III's arrival from Naples with his own team of architects, he was removed from the royal works.

What descriptive terms can be applied to the two periods extending over 1680 to 1770? Are they wholly related to Baroque or are there times when it is permissible to use the term Rococo as an autonomous style, as defined by Philippe Minguet? His definition calls for a suggested but unrealized architectural homogeneity, an envelope outlined but not bounded by considerations of intimacy, prettiness, and colour. These characteristics may be found here and there in the sacristy of the Cartuja at Granada and the sacramental chapel of the parish church of Priego in Andalusia by Pedraxas (1781) which continues the tradition of Hurtado in an exaggerated fashion; but the links are only fragmentary. Examples more in accord with Minguet's definition may be found in the royal palaces, notably the porcelain rooms at Aranjuez (1763–65) and the Royal Palace at Madrid (1765). Basically, however, the ceramic panelling of these two rooms is of Italian workmanship; Charles III had transported the entire El Retiro manufactory–men, machines and pastes–from Capodimonte to Madrid. Spanish architecture incorporated quite a few hints of Rococo but it was never a dominant influence. The term Baroque relates to the whole of its development.

Style in Spanish America

There is a marked scarcity of curved plans and undulating walls in Spanish America. It is possible to draw up only a very short list of not more than ten churches, five of which are, or were, in Mexico City or nearby. The Carmen church at San Angel by Fray Andrés de San Miguel (1577–1644) has a trefoil plan chapel, known as the chapel of Señor de Contreras, in the left arm of the transept, but the retables do not follow the movement of the walls. Santa María la Rotónda owes its name to a rotunda placed at the end of a long nave and inaugurated in 1735. The churches of the Hospital Real de Indios and of Santá Brígida (1740–44) were designed by Luis Díez Navarro before his departure for Guatemala in 1741; both have been destroyed and both were basically composed of graceful, harmonious curves. The Pocito Chapel at Guadelupe by Guerrero y Torres (1771–91) on the site of the miraculous fountain of the visions is directly inspired by a plan of an antique temple published by

Serlio; but this model was altered by the interplay of masses and domes. The Enseñanza church in Mexico City, attributed to the same architect (1772–78), keeps to straight lines, whilst hinting at a flexibility reminiscent of the Chapel. The church of the Hospital of San Vicente in El Salvador, which was possibly never completed, was in the style of Díez Navarro to whom it has been attributed. At Antigua in Guatemala, the novices' building of the Capuchin Convent (c. 1731) was circular in plan, without precedent either in Spain or in the New World. It has been suggested, but not proved, that the nuns made use of an old building housing public baths. In Lima are the tiny church of the Corazon de Jesus with its oval plan and cupola attributed to Cristobal de Vargas (1758–66) and the perfectly circular cloister of the Colegio de Santo Tomás (1783). At Cochabamba in Bolivia, the original church of the convent of Santa Teresa (c. 1753) consisted of a rectangular nave followed by a 'crucero' and a triangular 'presbiterio'; the roof of the nave fell in, however, before the 'crucero' could be vaulted, and it was rebuilt to a rectangular plan. The curve of the 'crucero' in the Jesuit church at Alta Gracia, Córdoba (Argentina), is echoed by the undulating wall. Such are the instances of curved plans; nevertheless they only concern a portion of the building and cannot always be considered Baroque.

Pocito Chapel, Guadalupe, Mexico, by Guerrero y Torres: plan

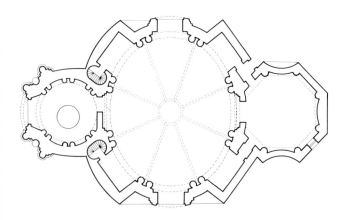

It is not so easy to prove that the architecture of South America does not incorporate several chapters of Hispanic art. Also it is necessary to disclaim a mother-daughter relationship between them, as Joseph Armstrong Baird has pointed out. What must be stressed is the parallel development between Spain and her various possessions.

A swift examination of style in the various regions reveals that the originality of the architecture is due to ornament rather than spatial conception.

In Cuba, especially in the prosperous 18th century, this resulted in remarkable buildings and pieces of town-planning, especially in Havana. Cuban decoration was relatively sober, owing to lack of feeling for

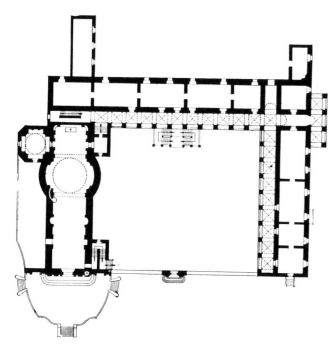

Jesuit Church at Alta Gracia, Córdoba, Argentina: plan (after Iñiguez)

New Granada, such a paradoxical opinion is untenable. The church of the Compañia in Quito was built in the 17th century in imitation of the Gesù, and its 18th century façade is of European inspiration and typically baroque in its splendour.

In the captain-generalcy of Guatemala there were no mines; wealth derived from agriculture and there were frequent earthquakes. Here there developed a simple style of church architecture with strong squat towers. The only indulgence lay in flat close-packed decoration with bosses and contrasting light and shade. Examples of this may still be seen at Antigua

Mérida Cathedral, Yucatán, 1563: longitudinal section and plan (after Kubler and Soria)

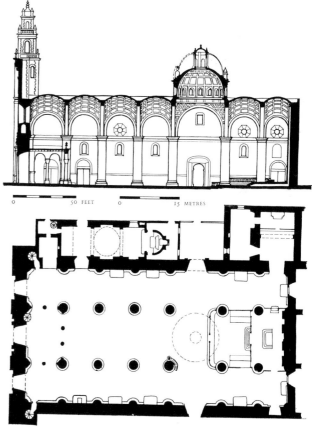

architecture among the islanders. Baroque here has been termed Borrominesque rather than Churrigueresque, not so much on account of the plans but because façades, such as that of Havana cathedral, and cornices with ascending, broken lines, are reminiscent of the architecture of S Carlo alle Quattro Fontane. Moreover, after 1760, the authority of architects from the region of Cadiz led to a revival of Italian influences.

In his study of the buildings of Venezuela, Graziano Gasparini shows that they derive from an uncomplicated, anonymous type of art and share simple plans and a restrained form of decoration except in the case of a few façades. He refuses to term them Baroque and extends this refusal to the whole of Hispano-American art.

In Ecuador which, with Venezuela, formed part of

in the frequently rebuilt churches of the Merced (c. 1650–90, 1767), San Francisco (1675–90, 1702), the Compañia (1695–98), and the Carmen (1728).

No artistic significance can be accorded to the territories of Rio de la Plata until the 18th century. In and around Buenos Aires at this period all the architects were either German or Italian; the chief architectural sites were in the hands of the Jesuits, who summoned their brethren from Bavaria, Tyrol and Lombardy. Even so, the style of building continued to be in a simple popular vein in contrast to the harmonious richness of the architecture of Mexico and Peru; it was vertical and flat with a fondness for prismatic masses. The Jesuits similarly impressed their characteristics on the tranquil Baroque of Córdoba, where remoteness and poor materials handicapped building; the finest piece of architecture there is the cathedral (1690–1758). The most important buildings are linked with the names of Jesuit brethren. San Ignacio in Buenos Aires was begun by Johann Kraus in 1712, and, in the same city, Andrés Blanqui was responsible for the Merced (1721–33), San Francisco (1730–54), Las Catalinas (1737–45) and the Cabildo (1725–65), churches which are now unfortunately disfigured or altered. Blanqui also completed the vaulting and built the main portal of Córdoba Cathedral after August 1729.

In the Jesuit reductions, extending over territories now forming part of the Argentine, Paraguay and Brazil, there were, of course, Spanish brethren, but, more particularly, Germans and Italians including Giovanni Battista Primoli (1673–1747) who arrived in Buenos Aires in 1717. At first the architecture was simple but became richer after the expulsion decreed by Charles III in 1767; at the same time, more attention was paid to the study of church plans and decoration – and to town-planning, on account of the Indian settlements which grew up round the churches.

The churches at Potosí, Chuquisaca (Sucre), Cochabamba, and La Paz, are notable for their decoration; their vernacular style which has often been remarked, is still more forcefully developed on the shores of Lake Titicaca at Puno, Juli, Pomata, and Zepita. All these towns formed part of Rio de la Plata, the last viceroyalty created by Madrid, but they also had regular contact with Peru.

In the viceroyalties of Peru and New Spain, Hispanic architecture of the baroque period made its individuality felt, perhaps less forcefully than around Lake Titicaca, but over wider areas and with increased richness; there were subtle regional variations in the exuberant decoration carpeting static surfaces.

In the northern Andean region of Peru, the three great churches at Cajamarca – the cathedral of Santa Catalina, San Antonio, and the Belém church – are remarkable for their façades dating from the first half of the 18th century. At Cuzco similar note should be taken of the façade of the Compañía built in the mid-17th century by Father Juan Bautista Egidiano, a Jesuit from Ghent, the main door of the cathedral probably by Francisco Domínguez de Chaves y Arellano (1651–7), the cloister of the Merced and the church of San Sebastián (1664–78). Solomonic columns copied from Bernini's may be identified in the door of the Sagrada Familia (1723, 1733–5). There is also a rare adoption of a central plan in the Triunfo by Fray Miguel de los Angeles Menchaca, who came from Spain as the bishop's major-domo; this may have been inspired by the 'Sagrario' of Granada cathedral (1732–5). The buildings of Arequipa owe their originality to their beautiful sculptures, which are on the surface and not recessed. The masterpiece of this local school is the church of the Compañía (1698) whose influence lasted for a whole century. At Lima the church of San Francisco was built after plans by the Portuguese architect Constantin de Vasconcelos (1657–73). The 18th century was ushered in with the church of Santa Rosa de las Monjas (1704–08); the building is completed by a later 'portada'. The city's baroque masterpiece is, as might have been expected, a façade – the 'portada' of San Agustín (1720). The Torre Tagle Palace, completed in 1735, owes its beauty not merely to its plan but also to its balconies and decorative sculpture.

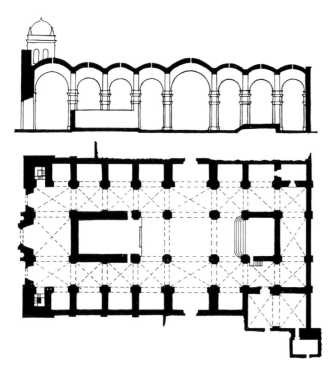

Cuzco Cathedral, 1582–1654: longitudinal section and plan
(after Kubler and Soria)

Architectural progression in all cities and regions of Mexico can be identified with reference to the development of ornament rather than plan. In the first stage up to about 1730, buildings were typified by undulating lines and the use of Solomonic columns. Pedro de Arrieta (d. 1738) built the church of the Profesa in Mexico City and the basilica of Guadelupe, and Miguel Custodio Durán was responsible for the churches of San Lázaro, San Juan de Dios and Santo Domingo. In the mid-18th century, the Solomonic column was replaced by the 'estípite'. Lorenzo Rodríguez, a native of Guadix, who came to New Spain after 1731, was its chief architectural exponent. From 1749 he built the 'Sagrario' of the cathedral in Mexico City, a central-plan building with two façades entirely streaked with 'estípites'. Outside the capital one must not always look for too strict an application of these stages. Those masterpieces of Mexican Baroque, the Jesuit colleges of Tepotzotlán and Santa Prisca at Taxco, built by Diego Durán between 1751 and 1759, imitated the taste of the capital. The region of Puebla, on the other hand, enjoyed its own strong artistic personality, and the interior decoration of buildings included many panelled enrichments reminiscent of the stucco decorations of Andalusia, the most astonishing example being the Rosary chapel of Santo Domingo (1650–90). The exteriors of cupolas were covered with ceramic tiles. San Francisco Acatapec and Santa Maria Tonantzintla outside the town both derive from a lyrical popular art form, and the church at Ocotlán, completed after delay in the 18th century, is a particularly original building – its pink towers rising from a narrower base contrasting with the gleaming whiteness of the 'imafronte'. At Oaxaca the baroque decoration of the cathedral façade is relatively severe, but the interior decoration of Santo Domingo reveals the influence of the stucco ornament of Santo Domingo at Puebla (after 1657); the decoration of the Rosary chapel was much later (1725–31). The church of the Valenciana near Guanajuato which was built by the generosity of a mine owner who died in 1786 before it was finished, surpasses those of the nearby town in elegance. In all this, preoccupations with space and volume were restricted to the few buildings already mentioned by Diéz Navarro and Guerrero Torres, to the plan of the 'Sagrario' at Mexico City by Lorenzo Rodríguez, and the adoption of the 'camarín' from Spain.

Conception of space in Spain and Spanish America

A study of style forces one continually to insist on the pre-eminence of ornament. Nevertheless, we should carry out a quick examination of the static structure of these buildings in its role of envelope. Church façades, whether they form a screen or a type of huge retable, are especially enhanced by decoration, and it is from this angle that they will receive further study. The customary silhouette with towers in the foreground and a dome behind helps to fill the surrounding space with verticals and vibrant colour. (In Mexico, however, domes were usually built without proper drums.) This outline modulates space and really belongs to the chapter devoted to town-planning.

What is now due for analysis are plans and masses, in other words the conception of space.

Churches of mudéjar origin with single elongated naves shaped into a cross by a transept had been popular in Andalusia and the design spread to America, where it may be found in Peru, Guatemala, and Mexico. Frequently enriched and developed it became the standard Hispanic church plan of the baroque period. With its simple design and its series of right angles, it could be broken up into prismatic masses and was ready to receive lavish decoration. Santa Prisca at Taxco is a perfect illustration of this type of church. The core of the building is a long nave separated by a short transept from the high altar set against the back wall. On either side of the nave walls are subsidiary constructions housing the chapel of the Indians, the baptistery, and an office. The sacristy and various rooms are placed to each side of and behind the high altar. The construction of this type of church may be termed static. To find the Baroque here we must, in the words of Pierre Charpentrat, 'endeavour to obtain the flavour of the almond by gnawing the shell'. Perhaps we have made too strict a division between structure and ornament. Supposing the essence of the building lies in its decoration rather than in its structure, must not the former influence one's view of the latter?

One of the characteristics of baroque architecture is the more or less blurred envelope of the building and its divisions. This feature is usually obtained by the modulation of the envelope – in other words, the walls, vaults and domes. It may be argued that a similar effect is produced in Hispanic buildings with their static structure by gilded wood retables, stuccoes, plaster decoration ('yeserías'), marbles and painting. If, in our mind's eye, we strip off this decoration, we are left with a bare building, a notable example of the divided prismatic conception of Spanish architecture. If we restore the decorations, they mask or blur this envelope, substituting vibrant colours for the harshness of lines and angles.

In northern Spain at the start of the 17th century, the accepted models were no longer the great Gothic cathedrals of Segovia and Salamanca, but Juan de Herrera's project for Valladolid (c. 1585), with its four corner towers and its wide central nave. Although it remained unfinished, it inspired the design for the new cathedral of the Pilar at Saragossa (c. 1675) by a local architect, Felipe Sanchez; he proposed four corner towers, three naves, and a dome near the altar. Francisco Herrera the younger, who took over in 1680, revised this project, giving it the symmetry called for by its site on the Ebro, and conceiving the side aisles as vast circulatory spaces surrounding the central area reserved for the high altar, the canons' choir, and the chapel of the apparition of the Virgin to St James. Instead of designing a single space and then dividing it with 'trascoro' and 'trasaltar', he set about planning a multiplicity of spaces from the start. He was, in fact, bearing in mind a constant of Hispanic architecture. The only sign of the Baroque in his project lay in the taste for the monumental. Its dominance increased, however, with later modifications, especially those of Ventura Rodríguez from 1750 onwards, and with the addition of sumptuous decoration.

The majority of the great cathedrals in America were begun in the 16th century and modelled on those of Andalusia – Seville, Granada, and Jaén. They inclined to Baroque either by a gradual change of course or by employment of ostentatious ornament. The only churches in this style are the cathedral at Buenos Aires by Masella, except for its neo-classic façade; the cathedral at Córdoba, built under difficult circumstances between about 1690 and 1758, and that at Potosí designed by Fray Manuel de Sanahuja (1809–36).

It was left to the town of Cadiz to provide the finest design for a Hispanic baroque cathedral. This prosperous port and city demanded a building worthy of its new-found importance. The plans drawn up by

Vicente d'Acero y Arebo in 1725 are known from a group of drawings revealing the twin sources of Spanish Plateresque and Italian Baroque. Acero was inspired by the chevet of Granada cathedral, but aimed for a more open, more luminous, composition. With extreme cleverness he combined straight lines with convex and concave masses. The dome was to be 85 metres (247 feet) high with an interior height of 32 metres (105 feet), more than at Seville cathedral; nave, 'crucero', choir rotunda and camarín were all to be of different heights producing a picturesque effect; the towers were to be equal in height to the length of the church (100 metres, 110 yards) and would have surpassed the Giralda at Seville; they were to be set on pedestals of four storeys and their huge belfries would have included two storeys.

The crypt and foundations are the work of Acero himself, but the realization of the entire project required too much time and money. Faced with the technical difficulties of the dome (1727–30), Pedro de Ribera and Leonardo de Figueroa were asked for their opinion. Acero left the site in 1729 and the building of the cathedral continued very slowly; the design was pruned and altered and the dome was not constructed until the 19th century, rising to a height of 47.5 metres (157 feet) instead of the planned 85. The towers do not equal the building's total length, but only half of it; the number of storeys was reduced and the belfries, together with the attic, were built in the neo-classic style. The picturesque variations in height of the 'camarín', the rotunda, the cupola and the towers have been simplified. Nevertheless, the cathedral of Cadiz, especially the interior, makes a striking impression with its majestic sense of movement and noble luminosity.

The spread of the Jesuit Order was not automatically accompanied, as has long been believed, by the adoption of the design of the Gesù in Rome. The Order

Cadiz Cathedral: longitudinal section (after O. Schubert)

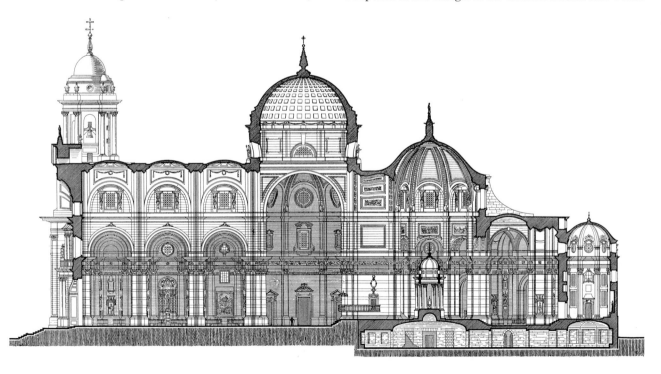

merely required its churches to profit from a number of characteristics related to the needs of religious life. These included free standing, easily visible altars, a suitable pulpit, galleries for the clergy and their students leaving the nave of the church to the general public, side chapels for the celebration of the Mass, and oratories giving directly on to the altar where the clergy could pray without being seen. The Gesù's interior is the result of a reconciliation between the ideas of Giovanni Tristano and Vignola, but the façade was executed according to the designs of Giacomo della Porta. In many respects this church was the one best suited to these diverse needs. Nevertheless, the type was not systematically imposed; local contingencies and economic necessities were too strong. Pierre Moisy has shown that the Jesuits of the Assistance de France enjoyed great architectural freedom and that the most famous of their architects, Brother Martellange, took his inspiration not so much from the Gesù as from Giacomo della Porta's S Maria dei Monti. The Order neither invented nor enforced Jesuit or baroque art, but declared its preference for a type of church ideally exemplified by the Gesù.

This was indeed the case in Spain where this type was usually adopted and helped the spread of the Baroque, but it was diversified with individual variations as a few notable examples will show. In the Clerecía at Salamanca, Juan Gómez de Mora designed the Fathers' cells in accordance with a strict geometrical pattern. The layout of the Gesù is plainly echoed in his plan for the church and in its interior, but the 'trascoro' of the clergy is situated behind the altar in accordance with the pattern set by Juan de Herrera in Santa María de la Alhambra and the cathedral at Valladolid. Of Bautista's two churches, the one at Toledo is closer to Italian models. His Madrid church reveals an increasing detachment from the model of the Gesù. The massive façade with its projecting towers is explained by the influence of Giacomo della Porta; the connection between the components of the nave is better arranged, for the great arcades alternate harmoniously with embrasures introduced between the pairs of pilasters. The false wooden cupola ('cúpula encamonada') together with the towers makes up a highly successful silhouette. On the other hand, the Jesuits agreed to abandon their usual models in the church of San Luis at Seville. Leonardo de Figueroa took as his inspiration for the lower portion of the façade and the central plan Rainaldi's project of 1652 for S Agnese in Piazza Navona. Four semicircular chapels radiate from the central cupola and between them are set small apses of similar shape.

It would be an exaggeration to say that the Gesù was never imitated in Spanish America. Despite some variations, it provided the inspiration for San Ignacio in Buenos Aires begun by Brother Kraus in 1712 and for the Compañía at Arequipa (1590–1660?). There are, especially, frequent examples of variations. The church of San Francisco Javier at Tepotzlán is built in the shape of a Latin cross, has a single nave and no galleries. Galleries are also lacking in the Compañía at Quito which nevertheless follows the plan of the Gesù.

In his use of a central plan in San Luis at Seville, Leonardo de Figueroa showed himself an innovator, although he was adopting an old model. Leaving out the subtle plan of the Bernardas church at Alcalá de Henares with its four oval chapels set around a central oval space, we must wait for the 18th century for this type of plan to become more common. The square central plan used by Hurtado in the 'Sagrario' of the Cartuja at Granada allowed multiple perspectives without damaging the integral appearance of the building, but it only became fully baroque with the expansion of the decoration as is revealed in the 'Sagrario' of the cathedral in Mexico City where Rodríguez imitated Hurtado. Now, stripped of its ornament, the interior has become a mere sketch of itself, which it is difficult and perhaps impossible to clarify as belonging to one style rather than another. Pedro de Ribera's hermitage of the Virgen del Puerto is an entirely different matter. The lozenge-shaped plan bulges outwards at the corners to form four half circles; towards the back, two circular chambers are separated by a raised 'camarín'. Nevertheless, the

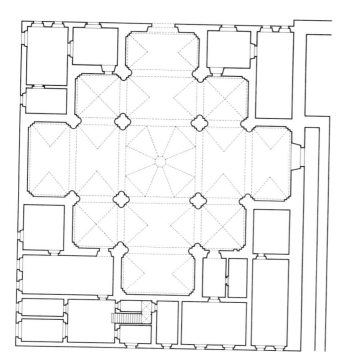

Sagrario of Mexico City Cathedral, by Rodriguez

by the mass of the dome, a concave cup shedding a theatrical light.

The 'Sagrarios', in honour of the Holy Sacrament, are more subtly varied in volume and plan and are often more richly decorated, deriving from the florid Baroque. Huvtardo designed one at the Cartuja of Granada as the circular envelope of the 'Transparente', in this case a huge baldacchino surrounded by niches and their framing columns. The design at El Paular is on a grander scale as behind the chamber of the 'Transparente' there extends a larger cross-shaped room whose arms comprise circular chapels; between them are built four other chapels, also circular. At Tepotzotlán in Mexico a combination of the 'camarín' and the cult of the Casa de Loreto resulted in the building of a Santa Casa at the side of the church; it was bordered by two corridors enclosing a polygonal rotunda. Thus, the whole composition was solely made up of simple masses and

Chapel of San Antonio, Aranjuez, by Bonavia (after O. Schubert)

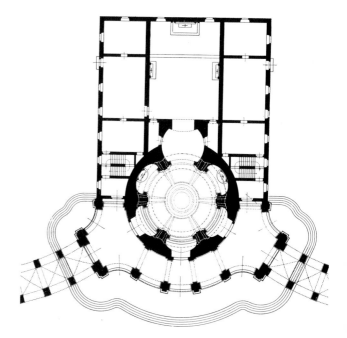

outline remains Hispanic thanks to the composition of the towers and dome and the definition of the envelope. From the outside all these components assume prismatic facets. In the case of Bonavía's churches of San Miguel at Madrid and San Antonio at Aranjuez and in Ventura Rodríguez's church of San Marcos at Madrid, on the other hand, supple lines and shapes in the Italian fashion enfold the masses rising from the central plan.

The 'camarín' is one of the most Hispanic features of baroque architecture. One of the earliest and richest is at the Virgen de los Desamparados in Valencia. In a complex manner it unites spaces which are essentially simple. The oval-shaped chapel is set within a rectangular building and is dominated by the small square chamber of the 'camarín', reached by two flights of a staircase situated to the rear. The interplay of the various spaces is supplemented plans, prismatic in accordance with the Spanish fashion, but combining to be favourable to surprise and lavish decoration.

Because of their sites in towns and gardens, the royal palaces are partially related to town-planning. Private palaces set around patios and colleges distributed around interior courts give scant indications in their plans – except at Loyola – of belonging to the baroque period. This makes itself particularly felt in monumental grandeur, the desire for majestic enfilades of rooms, and the theatrical design of staircases. As part of his work for the king, Velázquez designed the octagonal saloon and the hall of mirrors in the Alcázar at Madrid. In an unexecuted project for the Royal Palace, Pedro de Ribera devised a number of polygonal rooms in a symmetrical plan. In the present Royal Palace and at Aranjuez, Sacchetti and Bonavía built staircases with multiple flights for the display of court processions. Sacchetti's was unfortunately replaced under Charles III with a more constricted design by Sabatini.

Architectural analysis of buildings in Portugal and Brazil

Portuguese builders instinctively conceived clearcut masses and discarded buildings with excessively complex articulation. Their ideal consisted of a rectangular church with a sloped roof covering the various areas needed for worship and free circulation; these adjacent sections were not separated by arcades, but by actual walls, resulting in a partitioned church related to those built in Georgia and Armenia in the Early Christian period. Portuguese temperament found its preferred outlet in Romanesque architecture; the influence of the Romanesque continued for a long time, for its success was more than a purely stylistic matter – it expanded throughout the country as a permanent spiritual need.

This national proclivity provided the Jesuits with freer inspiration for their early churches begun before the erection of the Gesù in 1578. They gave up building domes and, taking as their model São Francisco at Evora by Martin Lourenço (1460–1501), elaborated a type exemplified by the churches of São Roque at Lisbon (1565–73), the Espírito Santo at Evora (1567–74), and São Paulo at Braga (1567–88). These are rectangular in plan with a single nave sometimes lined with side-chapels; if there is a transept it is embedded in the building and does not appear as an exterior feature; the same applies to the 'capela-mór' which, at the most, only appears as a slight external projection.

This tradition of simple, compactly planned buildings clashed with the innovations which arrived from Spain and Italy in the late 16th century and included the new ideas of Juan de Herrera. Italy was the native country of the military engineer Filippo Terzi, architect at São Vicente de Fora at Lisbon, begun in 1582. From Italy he borrowed the Latin cross plan, the dome over the transept crossing, the rich façade with its three storeys and many windows, and the decorative detail. In its general austerity, however, it recalls Spanish architecture and borrows from Juan de Herrera – at Santa María de la Alhambra and in the design for Valladolid cathedral – the positioning of the monks' choir behind the altar and possibly above the vestibule-narthex.

Thus the 17th century inherited a twofold example quite independent of the regaining of political autonomy in 1640, an event which caused no break in artistic development. On the one hand was the taste for simple compact buildings, on the other Italian and Spanish influences broadly interpreted and not confined to the single obsessive model of the Gesù.

The Jesuit churches provide a convincing set of proofs in this field. The collegiate church at Coimbra records the foreign connections – a dome surmounting a Latin cross, a transept as high as the centre vault – but there are no galleries. The building was begun in 1598, the nave was inaugurated in 1640 and in its original state the 'capela-mór' was very shallow. After the expulsion of the Order, however, the building became a cathedral and was lengthened by two bays on the side of the high altar to accord with its

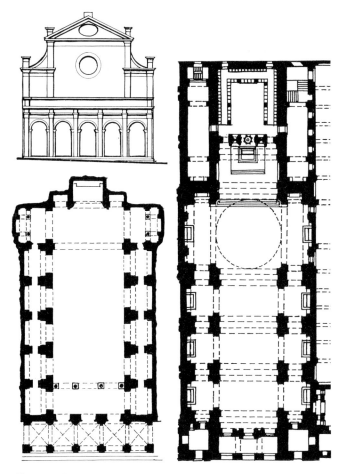

Church of Espírito Santo, Evora, 1567 (left): elevation and plan
São Vicente de Fora, Lisbon, 1582 (right): plan (after Kubler and Soria)

national standards predominate in the collegiate church at Santarém. The Espírito Santo at Evora served as a model for the plan approved at Rome on 15th July 1673; the transept was to remain lower than the lofty vault and was included in the plan; the building was completed for worship in 1687, both transept and towers were abolished, and the side chapels became mere niches set in the depth of the wall. The Espírito Santo at Evora was also, to a lesser degree, the model for the collegiate church of São Salvador at Elvas (1679–92).

The churches with unified designs and cellular envelopes built during the second half of the 17th and the early part of the 18th centuries can also be related to this taste for compact plans. The convent church of Santa Clara-a-Nova at Coimbra (1649–96), probably designed by the Benedictine João Turriano (1610–79), is a striking example of concentrated composition; a rectangular envelope enfolds the nuns' choir on two levels, the nave for public worship, and the sanctuary with rooms closely nested around it.

This plan clearly reveals the interest in structure peculiar to Central and Southern Portugal, whereas the interest of the North was centred on ornament.

Motifs by Wendel Dietterlin and Vredeman de Vries provided inspiration for the decoration of the Grilos and Carmo churches (1619–28, 1650) at Oporto; the accentuation of the division of sections and storeys in the former produces a more startling contrast of light and shade than in the Angustias church at Valladolid or in the 'Sagrario' at Seville. The flowering of powerful motifs continues to increase on the façades of the Congregados (1657–80) at Oporto, and of São Victor (consecrated in 1686) and the Franciscanos (consecrated 1691) at Braga. Then, in the 18th century, Niccolò Nasoni introduced Southern Italian Baroque to Oporto: he was a native of Fiesole, but had probably worked in Lecce and Malta. For a long time the cathedral loggia with its strongly defined decoration was attributed to him. São Pedro dos Clérigos is undoubtedly his design and his masterpiece (1732–56), and analysis will reveal its complex

new use. The Coimbra church served as a model for the collegiate church of São Lourenço, better known as Os Grilos, at Oporto; this was begun in 1614 by Baltasar Álvares and practically finished in 1622. Instead of a dome, however, it has a ribbed vault with studded tracery. The domed plan was adopted for the collegiate church built at Beja in the late 17th century and for São Bartolomeu, the church of the Casa Professa at Vila Viçosa, both of which have now been turned into markets. Unlike these buildings, character. The main façade with its staircase recalls the work of Fernando de Casas y Novoa at Santiago. The tower at the rear (1754) is in the traditional style of the region of Braga, but its design is reminiscent of Contini's tower at the old cathedral of Saragossa. The design of the interior, with the oval nave em-

Church of São Pedro dos Clérigos, Oporto, by Niccolò Nasoni, 1732 (left): plan
São Salvador Cathedral, 1657 (right): section and plan (after Kubler and Soria)

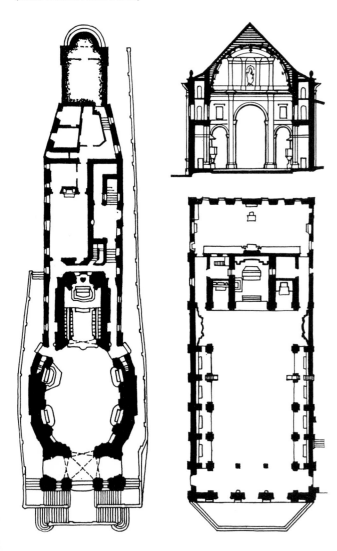

phasizing the narrowness of the sanctuary surrounded by three corridors, is Portuguese in style.

It is significant that the Theatine Guarino Guarini was responsible for the plan of Santa Maria Divina Providência (1652–3), the church of his Order in Lisbon. It was destroyed in the earthquake of 1755, but is known from engravings in his posthumous treatise, the 'Architettura Civile' (1737). The longitudinal plan rejected any suggestion of a straight line except in the two sacristies flanking the sanctuary and the exterior envelope of the chevet. Everywhere else, below the domes, the vibrant movement of circular volumes overflowed into neighbouring divisions: the two bays of the nave expanded into the side chapels and the oval transept and sanctuary opened out in a semicircle beyond a convex bottleneck with two hollow niches.

This was an importation of unadulterated Italian Baroque. There are also other examples showing a combination of foreign influences and national tendencies. In 1682 João Nunes Tinocco produced an unexecuted design for Santa Engrácia in Lisbon based upon S Agnese in the Piazza Navona. Another of his plans consisted of a vast hexagonal hall clasped among four corner towers and provided with corridors reserved for the clergy. The unfinished church was continued by João Antunes. The corridors sprang from Portuguese originality, but the great central space was a reversion to the Greek-cross plan of Bramante's St Peter's.

The gold of Brazil provided the courts of John V and Joseph I with the means to indulge in a lavish style of architecture, until the rebuilding of Lisbon brought about the development of a more simple, almost functional type of construction related to town-planning. Johann Friedrich Ludwig became the favourite architect of John V under the name of Ludovice: he had been born at Hall in Swabia about 1672, had become a goldsmith in Rome, and worked under Andrea Pozzo on the altar of St Ignatius in the Gesù. The building of Mafra so skilfully analysed by George Kubler reveals his talent and the complexity of the official baroque style far more than the choir of Evora cathedral or the University Library at Coimbra, whose chief interest lies in its elegant interior decoration. The vast scale of the buildings which were begun in 1717 recalls the Escorial, but this is the only feature shared by the two edifices. Philip II's creation was primarily a monastery, the palace was thrown to one side behind the church. The basilica at Mafra, on the other hand, is incorporated in the palace, which occupies the main front, while the monastery has been relegated to the rear. This arrangement indicates German influence as do the end pavilions with their fortress bases and bulbous caps. Nevertheless, many more features are of Italian inspiration. The influence of Carlo Fontana as much as of Central European monastic architecture lies behind the positioning of the church in the centre of the façade (his plan for Loyola) and the bulbous spires (his church of S Maria dei Miracoli). The wings connecting the end pavilions to the church derive from the Montecitorio façade, and the front of the church from the loggia of St Peter's by Maderna. The concavely curved drum and dome spring from Borromini and the Doric arcades of the nearby courtyard from S Maria in Transtevere. Finally, the Italian love of richness is linked to Portuguese taste in the marbled interiors. This taste, apparently abandoned in favour of foreign influences, reappears in the multiplicity of galleries at different levels in the church, in the exaggerated size of the windows, especially in the oval chapter-room, and in the walls and vaults of brick plastered over and decorated with marble and limestone.

Such subtleties reveal the maintenance of nationalistic tendencies. They are even more strongly marked at the Queluz Palace, where Ludovice's pupil Mateus Vicente de Oliveira was responsible for the northern nucleus of the buildings (1747–52); the western pavilion is by the French architect Jean Baptiste Robillion.

The designs of Carlos Mardel, a Hungarian who arrived in Lisbon in 1733, were not so elaborate as those of Ludovice and were favourably received in the Portuguese capital. He introduced a greater subtlety with his dynamic scalloped plans and even took Chinese curved roof edges as models.

The contrast between Northern Portugal where interest was centred on decoration and Central and Southern Portugal where structure was considered more important carried over to Brazil, where Bahia became known as the 'black Rome' and Rio de Janeiro adopted the Neo-Classic style from Lisbon. The trend towards compact plans perhaps found more typical expression than in Portugal in the former Jesuit church of São Salvador (1657–72), later the cathedral. The façade was modelled on that of São Vicente de Fora in Lisbon, and the interior was inscribed within a rectangle under a sloped roof. This was divided so as to form the 'capela-mór' and its side chapels; the sacristy occupied the entire rear of the building, the transept was raised to the level of the upper vaulting, and the nave was closely surrounded by chapels and galleries. The facing of limestone brought from Lisbon afforded additional proof of the Portuguese character of this Brazilian church.

Some details of architectural design imported from Portugal found their most original expression in Minas Geraes in the second half of the 18th century. They included towers recessed behind façades as presaged at the Grilos in Oporto, unified naves, and circular envelopes. Five churches which have been the subject of a detailed study by Yves Bruand are especially worthy of note. Two of them are attributed to António Pereira de Souza Calheiros – the Rosario Chapel at Ouro Preto (1753–85) and São Pedro dos Clérigos at Mariana. The latter was founded by Don Manuel de Cruz, first bishop of the town (1748–64), but the 'capela-mór' was probably not roofed until 1773 and the façade was not completed until the twentieth century. Behind the façade, which consists of a central convex section between two recessed towers, are two ellipses corresponding to the nave and the 'capela-mór'. In the Rosary Chapel these ellipses are surrounded by corridors giving access to the rectangular sacristy situated at the rear of the building. In São Pedro dos Clérigos, however, only

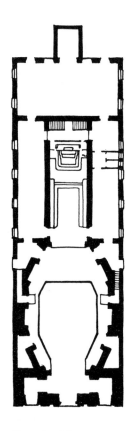
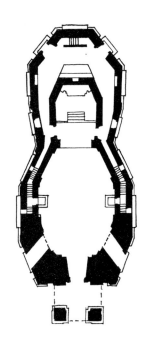

Church of São Pedro dos Clérigos, Recife, 1728 (left): plan
Church of Nossa Senhora de Glória do Outeiro, 1733 (right):
plan (after Kubler and Soria)

the sanctuary is surrounded by corridors.

The three remaining churches are by António Francisco Lisboa (1738–1814), son of the architect Manuel Francisco Lisboa and a coloured woman. Being a mulatto he could not initiate contracts himself and he was also the victim of a type of leprosy which left him a cripple; hence his customary name of Aleijadinho. Despite this, he was the greatest Brazilian artist – both a sculptor of almost primitive power and an architect of outstanding taste. His plan for São Francisco at Ouro Preto dates from 1766, the design for the façade was altered in 1774, and the building and decoration of the church lasted from

1766 to 1794. His father produced a plan for Nossa Senhora do Carmo in the same town in 1766, but Aleijadinho modified it in 1770–1 and gave the church a curved outline; building lasted until 1795. His plans for São Francisco at São João d'El Rei date from 1774, but the façade was modified by Francisco de Lima Cerqueira and the church completed shortly before 1810. In these three buildings, the towers are recessed in relation to the façades, movement is stressed, especially in São Francisco at Ouro Preto, and façade decoration, though rich, does not alter the balance of the structure. A rectangular plan is combined with curved outlines; the nave narrows towards the towers and helps to emphasize them; the 'capela-mór' and sometimes the nave are surrounded by long corridors. In São Francisco at São João d'El Rei, Aleijadinho abandoned the compact plan, squaring off the nave on the entrance side and curving it towards the sanctuary, whilst sanctuary and sacristy are included in an elongated rectangle. It is quite possible, as Yves Bruand suggests, that Aleijadinho was aware of António de Lima Calheiro's double elliptical plans and, reacting as a sculptor rather than as an architect, borrowed them not so much from wishing to modify the traditional rectangular block as out of a desire to make use of the curving envelope to enhance the decoration.

Experts on Luso-Brazilian architecture prefer to associate it with Mannerism, Classicism and Rococo rather than with Baroque. Indeed, the term Rococo may well be applied to the graceful palace of Queluz and to some intimate florid churches with ill defined interior boundaries like those designed by Aleijadinho. Love of façade decoration, especially in Northern Portugal, the projects for Santa Engracia, and the designs of Ludovice and Nasoni, are to a great extent related to Baroque, but this style is especially evident in interior decoration.

In Iberian and Ibero-American countries, the baroque conception of space is seldom found and is often related to foreign influence, but the most obviously prismatic spaces are polluted by decoration, and it is to this that we must now turn.

Plates

Granada

107 The Cartuja, general view of the church and its ancillary buildings. Far right, the sacristy. Centre, the Sagrario or Sancta sanctorum behind which is the church itself. Left, the patio.

108 The patio, very simple with its Doric order (17th century).

109 Apse of the church, interior. With regard to the baroque decoration, note the ornamentation of the walls by Díaz de Rivero (1662) with its inclusion of Mannerist motifs, and the baldacchino of the altar (1710) sheltering a wooden figure of the Virgin by José de Mora. The paintings are by Sánchez Cotán and Bocanegra.

110 Upper portions of the apse of the church.

111 Sacristy, looking towards the altar. Decorated with 'yeserías' and costly materials, this was executed between 1727 and 1764.

112 Sacristy, detail.

113 Sacristy, detail.

114 Sagrario, dome. In Hurtado's 'Sagrario', Palomino painted the dome with a 'Triumph of the Eucharist' (1712).

Ocotlán

115 Sanctuary of Ocotlán, façade of the church. The building stands to the rear of a huge square or atrium. It makes a striking impression with its contrasting colours (white, with red bricks set flat) and with the explosion of decoration.

116 Central section of the façade or 'imafronte', detail: an archangel.

117 Upper portions of the façade. Note both the key position accorded to the Virgin in the centre of the star-shaped rose-window.

118 Dome of the church.

Taxco

119 Santa Prisca. Central section of the façade or 'imafronte'. In accordance with the traditional layout, the 'imafronte' is set between two towers. The exuberant ornament is matched by a certain clarity of design. The bas-relief represents the Baptism of Christ between statues of the two saints to whom the church is dedicated – SS Prisca and Sebastian.

120 Retable of the high altar. The main theme is the Christian Church. In the sections seen here, note the triumph of the Church manifested through the glory of the Virgin (painting of the Immaculate Conception, in the centre, set in a niche subsequent to the execution of the retable) and through the martyrs (Sebastian and Prisca, whose statues are placed on either side of the painting). In the upper portions, St Peter and two popes represent the primacy of the Vicar of Christ. The Eternal Father crowns the retable and watches over the Church.

121 Detail of the retable of Our Lady of Guadalupe; the two angels are set at the feet of a saint in the guise of a bishop.

La Paz

122 San Francisco. Detail of the central 'portada' of the façade. The church of the monastery of San Francisco derives from the so-called mestizo architecture found on the shores of Lake Titicaca; the primitive decoration is exuberant, stylised and close set and the natives played a large part in its execution. The columns of San Francisco with their spiral decoration and representations of leaves are similar to some executed several years earlier at the church of Santiago in Pomata.

123 Detail of the central 'portada' of the façade. Several human heads similar to the one shown here are placed below the columns.

124 The nave. Architectural interest is limited here.

125 The dome with one of its pendentives. The decoration of the dome, like that in Santiago at Pomata, is suggestive of an Indian dance.

126 Central section of the dome.

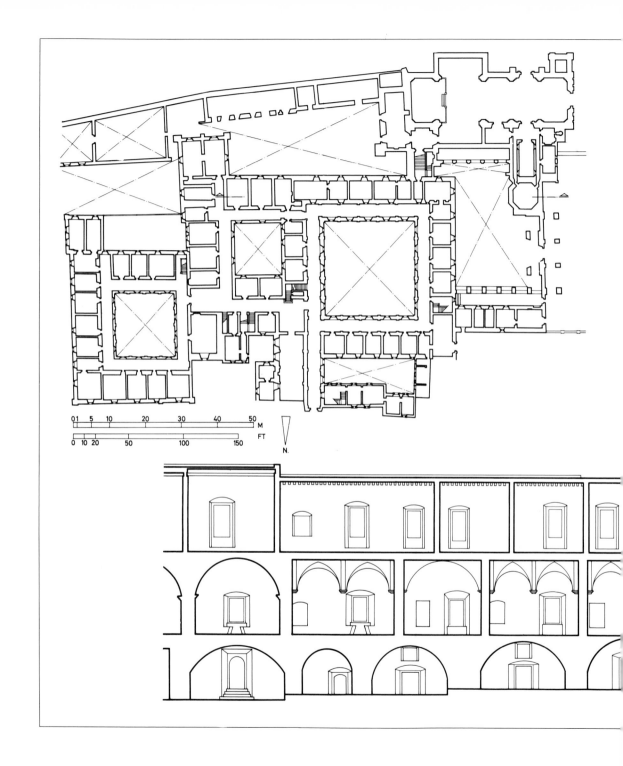

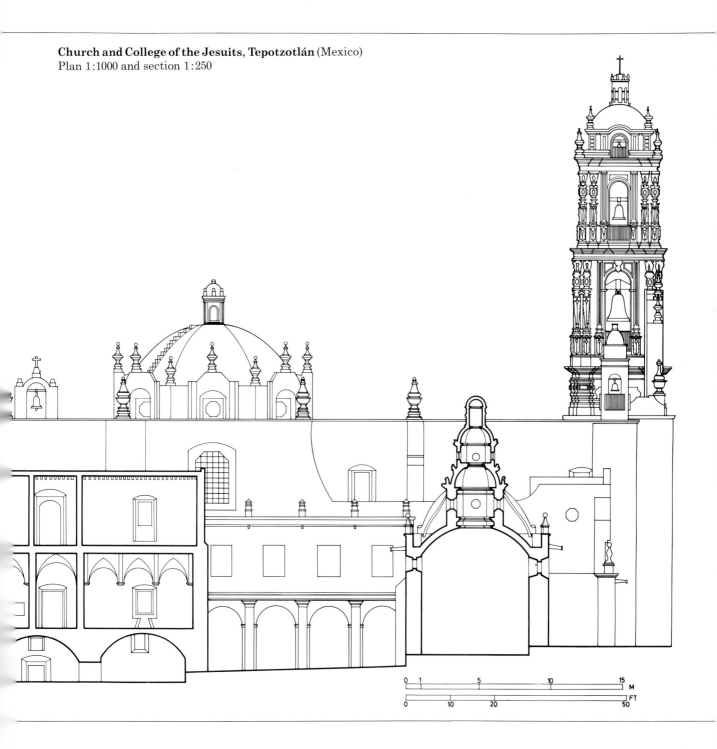

Church and College of the Jesuits, Tepotzotlán (Mexico)
Plan 1:1000 and section 1:250

0 1　　　　5　　　　　　10　　　　　　15
　　　　　　　　　　　　　　　　　　　M
0　　　　10　　　20　　　　　　　　　50
　　　　　　　　　　　　　　　　　　　FT

Notes

Granada

Cartuja. This was founded in 1506; in 1516, it was transferred to its present site and was partially destroyed in 1842. There now remain a 17th-century patio decorated with episodes from the life of St Bruno and the Carthusian martyrs by Vicente Carducho and Brother Juan Sánchez Cotán; several monastic rooms; the church tower and, finally, the church itself with its Sagrario and sacristy illustrating three stages of Spanish baroque architecture in its most decorative and lavish aspects. The church was begun in the mid-16th century, but building was interrupted and it was not completed until the first third of the 17th century; it is of special note for its interior decoration in which Díaz de Rivero brought the favourite mannerist motifs of Andalusia to their baroque flowering (1662). The 'Sagrario', lined with costly materials and housing the lofty 'Transparente' below Palomino's 'Triumph of the Holy Sacrament', is by Hurtado; it was completed in 1720 and heralds the florid baroque style which is developed in the sacristy. This was not completed until 1764. The church, 'Sagrario' and sacristy are decorated with numerous baroque paintings and sculptures. The chancel separating the choir of the brothers from that of the Pathers is by the lay brother José Manuel Vázquez (1750).

Ocotlán

The sanctuary of Ocotlán owes its origin to the repeated appearances of the Virgin to an Indian in 1541 or 1561; the Virgin took the form of a sculpture placed in a tree. These apparitions were very similar to those at Tepeyac which were the origin of the cult of the Virgin of Guadalupe near Mexico City. In both cases the name of the Indian was Juan Diego. The pilgrimage of Ocotlán was entrusted to the Franciscans. The present church built by the parish priest Juan de Escobar for the pilgrimage of 1691 is the successor to the early sanctuary. Built to a cruciform plan, it has survived only in so far as its outline and walls are concerned. Father Manuel Loaizaga who arrived at Ocotlán in 1716, noted that the Virgin was already honoured by a retable, and constructed the 'camarín' behind the high altar; he also chose the theme of Pentecost to decorate the dome (1718–1723); the model for this was the Rosary Chapel in Santo Domingo at Puebla. The paintings of scenes from the life of the Virgin were executed by Juan de Villalobos, an artist from Puebla who died in 1724; the sculptures are by Francisco Miguel, an Indian from Tlaxcala. Miguel was also responsible for the retables of the 'presbiterio'; he died in 1749, so, despite the confirmation of Loaizaga, they were probably those preceding the existing ones which may be stylistically assigned to 1770–1780. The 'presbiterio' is completely lined with retables in accordance with the aesthetic defined by Francisco de la Maza. The façade is highly original on account of the white and red bricks and the upward surge of the belfries.

Taxco

Santa Prisca. This region is famous for its silver mines. Don José de la Borda devoted part of his immense profits from them to the erection of this church in which his son, Manuel, a priest, could celebrate the mass. The building is dedicated to St Sebastian and St Prisca, the latter a young martyr of the Roman nobility, put to death about 268–270, and was decorated and completed in a few years (1751–1759) under the auspices of Don José himself. This is the reason why its lavish Baroque obeys the need for architectural and decorative cohesion and represents aristocratic rather than ecclesiastical taste. Buildings undertaken by the clergy usually took several generations to complete. The architect was Diego Durán, and Miguel Cabrera was responsible for several paintings in the church and the scenes from the life of the Virgin in the sacristy.

La Paz

Church of San Francisco. The foundation of the monastery of San Francisco is connected with that of La Paz (1549). The monastery buildings, with the exception of the main cloister, date from the 17th century and are of little interest. The church, on the other hand, on account of its architectural importance and its decoration, is one of the most significant buildings of the region round Lake Titicaca. Its resemblance to Santiago at Pomata has nothing to do with its actual construction (1743–1784; tower, 1885). San Francisco is composed of three naves with transept and dome, a rectangular 'capilla mayor', an arched vault over the nave and a domed vault on pendentives over the aisles; Santiago at Pomata has a single nave with side chapels. The decoration of the main façade of San Francisco with its three doors (1772–1783), and the dome derive from Santiago.

117

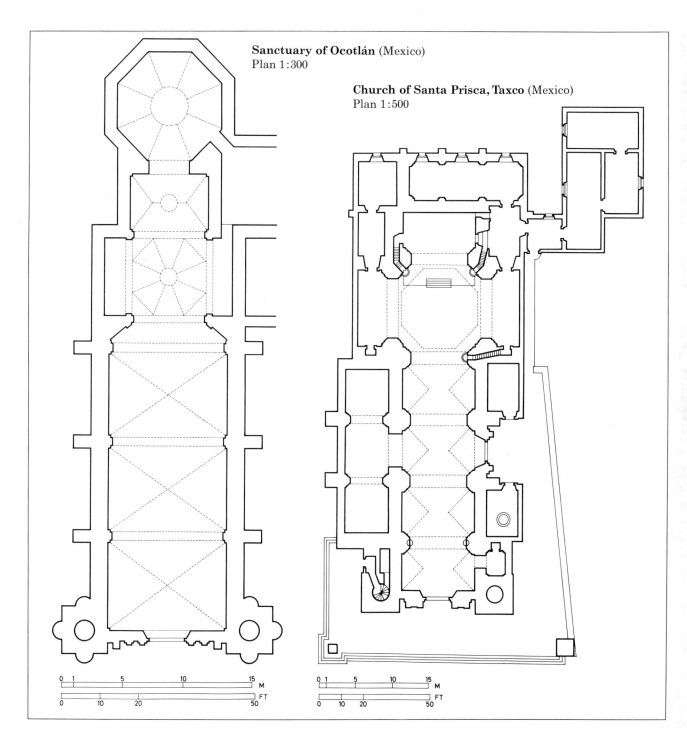

Sanctuary of Ocotlán (Mexico)
Plan 1:300

Church of Santa Prisca, Taxco (Mexico)
Plan 1:500

Church of San Francisco, La Paz (Bolivia)
Plan and elevation 1:400

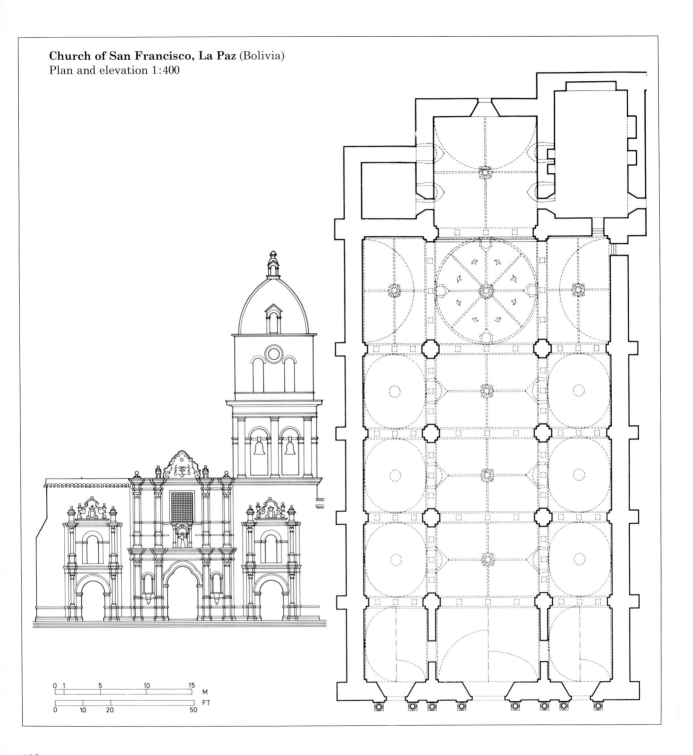

0 1   5   10   15   M
0   10   20   50   FT

4. Splendours of decoration

Varied materials, careful choice of plain and ornamented areas, rich iconography, and exuberant motifs, form the base for the decorative splendour which is the essential link of Iberian and Ibero-American architecture with the Baroque, apart from the few buildings previously surveyed in this book.

Materials and siting of decoration in Spain and Spanish America

The basic building material can contribute to the baroque effect by accentuating the architectural elements with contrasting light and shade; this is clearly seen in the façades of the Angustias at Valladolid and San Juan Bautista at Toledo. The brickwork is either left exposed or covered over with roughcast ('enfoscado'), a material capable of transforming pilasters, columns, pediments, and ornamentation. Thus the simple sculpture of fundamental materials detaches and refines the silhouettes of chevets, domes and towers, and, more especially, enables the central portion of the façade between the towers to be converted into a retable. In Galicia suitable decorative effects were obtained with granite, the hardness of the stone entailing the execution of solid large-scale motifs. At Oaxaca the greenish stone turns transparent when it rains. The great, fiery red 'portada' of the cathedral at Zacatecas is burnished or dulled according to the play of the sun on its various elements.

The use of different building materials, a simple enough device, could result either in muted or heightened colouring. At La Granja, a building typical of court art under Philip V, the Italian Sacchetti devised a subtle arrangement for the centre of the east façade overlooking the gardens: the pedestals of the giant order, the architrave and cornice are made of granite; white marble is used for capitals, vases, and the caryatids of the attic; the shafts of columns and pilasters and the frieze of the entablature are of red limestone from Sepúlveda. The simple red roof-tiles of Andalusia have a subtle sheen resembling that of plain brick. The architects of Mexico City experimented with a rather subdued polychromy com-

Reloj Tower, Santiago de Compostela Cathedral, by Domingo de Andrade: detail

bining red and black porous 'tezontle' with fine-grained light yellow Chiluca stone.

When the baroque freedom of effect was given its head, building materials were linked with the varied range of those required for ornamentation. In Northern and Western Spain this was usually restricted on the exterior to the subtle interplay of carved stone and in the interior to carved and gilded wooden retables rising as high as the vault. In Andalusia there was a fondness for brick facings roughcast in white below glazed roof-tiles. Andalusian church interiors offer unified painted decoration – marble either plain or as mosaic in the Italian manner, stucco, plaster expanding into statues, star-studded motifs and a multiplicity of ornamentation ('yeserías'), retables, and facings of square tiles. This varied repertory turns up again in Mexico, its most dazzling use being in the churches of Puebla and the surrounding area: domes are topped with rings of coloured tiles; inside, the 'yeserías' rise to the height of the vaults and are attached to exterior doors, windows and cornices. The façade of San Francisco Acatapec outside the town is completely faced with ceramic squares, that of Santa María Tonantzintla is partially covered with them. The sanctuary of Ocotlán in the same area is strikingly original in style: the centre of the façade and the upper half of the towers are gleaming white in contrast to the narrower bases of the towers which are covered with squares of brick.

Windows and doors often seem surrounded by overloaded frames contrasting with bare wall surfaces divided into geometrical compartments. The height of decorative development relates to doors: the 'portadas', both in secular buildings such as the Conde-Duque barracks in Madrid and in churches, are virtually transformed into retables, the most important usually being that of the main façade known in Mexico as the 'imafronte'. Decoration is also attached to the intersections of surfaces, the outlines of the overall plan, the caps of towers, and tiered divisions of the chevet and domes. Inside, the retables form the usual centres of the closed universe that is a baroque church. Occasionally, they take up whole walls, as in Santa Rosa at Morelia and Santa Clara and Santa Rosa at Querétaro where they are linked with a dazzling confusion of pictures and gilded wood. More often they are emphasized by the relative bareness of the walls or are linked by additional decoration of stucco, gilded wood or plaster motifs. The 'yeserías' may cover almost the entire surfaces of domes as in the sacristy of the parish church at Priego in Andalusia and especially at Puebla, the most notable example being the Rosary chapel of Santo Domingo. This type of 'yeserías' is also developed at Oaxaca in the Dominican church.

Decoration and iconography in Spain and Spanish America

Baroque is usually judged by the richness of its decoration and imagery, but this richness cannot be reduced to a chance interplay of shapes. After his revelation of the poetic clarity of medieval iconography, Émile Mâle realized to his surprise that another form of iconography, just as coherent, resulted from the Council of Trent; this was imposed by the Church and was expressed by painters and sculptors in accordance with exact directives. The artists of the 17th century were by no means indifferent to the sensual pleasure given by art – without it they would not have been artists – but they wished primarily to address themselves to intelligence and feeling. Subject was of prime importance both for them and the Church which supplied it to them.

The most widespread types of ornaments were not mere expressions of a desire for decorative profusion. Fruit, for instance, constituted an offering to God from man and a reminder of His benefits. Gold was more than a means of producing an effect of splendour – it was a symbol of divine light, previously used by the Incas. Mirrors, inset amid the decoration, multiply shapes and create a sensation of unreality.

Baroque iconography is to a great extent explained by reaction against Protestantism. It exalts the Eucharist, the Virgin, the Papacy, active charity, and the worship of saints.

In order to understand one of these mysterious new forms of devotion, we must revert to Émile Mâle. 'In 1516, in a Palermo church dedicated to St Ange, a martyr of the Carmelite Order, a strange fresco of seven archangels was uncovered from beneath a coating of whitewash. Three of them, Michael, Gabriel and Raphaël, had long been acknowledged by the Church, but four bore mysterious names unknown to regular worshippers: Uriel, Jehudiel, Barachiel and Sealtiel. In an inscription Michael was called "victoriosus", Gabriel "nuncius", Raphaël "medicus", Barachiel "adjutor" and Jehudiel "remunerator". They were also typified by attributes, some of which were puzzling. Michael, trampling Satan underfoot, carried a palm and a white standard with a red cross. Gabriel held a lighted lantern and a jasper mirror sprinkled with red spots. Raphaël bore a pyx and held the hand of young Tobias who carried a fish. Barachiel offered white roses in a fold of his cloak. Jehudiel held a gold crown in one hand and a whip trailing three black cords in the other. Uriel brandished a naked sword, and a flame sprang up before his feet. Finally, Sealtiel looked as if he was praying, with his hands crossed on his breast. It is possible to explain or at least to guess the meaning of these attributes. St Michael's standard bore witness to his victory over Satan. Gabriel held a lantern to light the way for travellers and on his mirror were recorded God's orders, intelligible only to himself. Raphaël, the healer, was typified by the pyx containing the precious ointments and by the fish which cured Tobias. The roses correspond to Barachiel's name which means "benediction of God". Jehudiel, "he who rewards", was shown carrying the crown of recompense and the whip of punishment. Uriel, "the powerful ally", had the sword and flame, and Sealtiel, "he who speaks", was addressing himself to God in an attitude of prayer.'

The iconographic programmes of the 'Transparente' in Toledo cathedral and the Sacristy of the Cartuja at Granada were pre-eminently inspired by the Eucharist.

The function of the 'Transparente' was to light the sacristy of the high altar and to recall the presence of the Host to the worshippers passing along the ambulatory. This explains the choice of themes for the several stages working upwards from the bottom: the Virgin and Child, or Jesus made man; the sun in clouds peopled by angels at the exact spot where its luminous rays penetrate to the sacristy through the Gothic vaults; the Last Supper and, still further above, the Trinity.

At the Cartuja the statues between the columns

supporting the dome represent chosen saints of the Carthusian Order: Joseph, the foster-father of Christ; Bruno, founder of the Order; the repentant Magdalene; John the Baptist, the forerunner dwelling in the wilderness. Above the circular windows are representations of the Virtues. Nevertheless, the cult of the Holy Sacrament forms the basis of the iconography in this place where it is kept. The 'Transparente' above the Host is surmounted by the image of the Faith and, at the corners, are gilded statues with the symbols of the Eucharist. Palomino who painted the dome has explained the symbolism of his work drawn from the Bible and Cesare Ripa's 'Iconologia'. The pendentives are occupied by the four Evangelists. At the base of the dome four scenes executed in shades of gold, surrounded by oval medallions and surmounted by large vases of flowers, are intermingled with four figures of Faith, monastic Religion, Silence, and Solitude. These scenes represent the Last Supper, Christ ministered to by angels in the wilderness, Christ in the house of Martha and Mary, and Christ and the pilgrims of Emmaeus. The actual drum is devoted to the Triumph of the Eucharist. This skilful, harmonious composition is centred on the monstrance placed on the terrestrial globe that is carried by the kneeling Saint Bruno, 'like a holy Atlas in this mystic heaven', in the words of Palomino.

At Seville, San Luis, the novitiate church of the Jesuits, displays some of their usual iconographical tendencies, stressing the roles of the Virgin, the angels, and the Eucharist, and honouring St Louis, the saints of the Company and other religious orders as well. The dedication of the church requires preliminary comment. The Jesuits wished to defend themselves in France against their reputation as teachers of regicide and so liked to dedicate their churches or at least an altar to St Louis. This custom probably took root in Spain after the accession of Philip V, grandson of Louis XIV; moreover, Louis IX was the cousin of Ferdinand of Castile who was canonized in 1671. In any case, he was chosen as patron of the church of the novitiate at Seville and the high altar was dedicated to him. On the exterior of the building terracotta statues of the Archangels Raphaël,

Michael and Gabriel are set above the portal. On the interior of the dome are sculptured representations of the Virtues distinguished by their Latin appellations: 'Charitas Dey', 'Paupertas', 'Obedientia', 'Mortificatio', 'Humilitas', 'Oratio', 'Castitas', and 'Charitas Proximi'. Below them are eight statues of the founder saints of religious orders. On either side of the main retable are altars placed under the patronage of famous Jesuit saints – on the left, Francesco Borgia, Ignatius Loyola and Louis de Gonzague; on the right, Stanislas Kotska, Francis-Xavier, and François Régis. An inscription reveals that the frescoes were executed under the direction of Domingo Martínez in accordance with a programme laid down by the former Superior Jerónimo de Hariza. Lucas Valdés, son of Valdés Leal, painted the vaults and on the dome portrayed the seven-branched candlestick, the shewbread, and the Ark of the Covenant. In the private chapel the places of honour on the retable were reserved for two young Jesuit saints, Louis de Gonzague and Stanislas Kotska.

Recent research into Mexican baroque iconography has yielded some interesting results. Monique Gustin, a young French art historian, has made a survey of eight country churches dating from the second half of the 18th century – the only link between them being the exposition of theological instruction provided by their façade decoration. They include San Salvador at Tzompatepec in the province of Tlaxcala, and San Francisco at Tilaco (1754–62) and San Miguel at Concá (1751–58) both in the province of Querétaro. They offer clear evidence of the overriding desire of the clergy to 'build churches in the smallest villages which were not only beautiful but endowed with a deep sensibility and language of their own.' The façades discussed have no trace of a taste for anecdote, of regional style, or of pre-Hispanic survivals capable of reminding their congregation of the gods and beliefs of their forefathers. Despite their architectural and decorative richness, new iconographic types are limited to the Virgin of Guadalupe, whose looks and native costume are really more of an adaptation than an innovation. This is an isolated example, for 'although one frequently sees representations of Christ with a gentle Indian look, religious art remains completely European in physical types, costume and tradition'. The Mexican influence on iconography is revealed in certain recurring points, including the place accorded St Peter and St Paul as representatives of the universality of the Church, and the Virgin usually portrayed as the Immaculate Conception, thus answering a deeply felt desire of the Indians 'brutally deprived of their gods'.

Constantino Reyes Valerio has made a detailed analysis of a group of churches situated in the neighbouring provinces of Morelos and Puebla. They cannot all be given an exact dating within the second half of the 18th century, but their common features are quite plain. The finest and most interesting is the sanctuary of Jesus Nazareno at Tepallingo, Morelos (26th February 1759 – 22nd February 1782), though it is not possible to fix its place in the overall chronology of the group. The 'imafronte' represents the fall of Man and his Redemption, the Passion of Christ and the spread of his teaching by the Apostles and Doctors of the Church, and the Last Judgment; this final theme includes the seven archangels so dear to the believers of the baroque period. A more or less similar blend of art and iconography may be found at four churches in the province of Puebla – Santa María and Santa Ana Jolalpan, San Lucás Tzicatlán and Santa María Tlancualpicán. This group constitutes an original chapter of Mexican Baroque. The iconographic themes which it offers must have come from Europe and been exploited by one or more priests who oversaw the building of the churches.

These two fields of enquiry indicate the vast results that may be achieved by future research. The best known Mexican baroque buildings, however, can reveal the development of baroque iconography in New Spain.

The most original and charming part of the interior decoration of Santa María Tonantzintla lies in the upper areas of the building; it hymns the graces and royal nature of the Virgin. The profusion of flowers may possibly hark back to pre-Hispanic times when the flower of the fields, the gift of the earth, symbolised the renewal of life; the 'flower of our flesh' was the maize which nourished it, and there was also the flower of the sacrifical victims who died in holocausts.

The sanctuary of Ocotlán is dedicated to the Virgin, who appeared there in conditions similar to those at Tepeyac; the pilgrimage was instituted by the Franciscans. With this in mind, the iconographical programme of the different parts of the building, though varying in merit, becomes clear. The late 18th century façade, the latest addition to the church, often makes one overlook the theme of the 'imafronte' on account of its strange beauty. The seven archangels with outspread wings occupy the niches of the 'estípites' and the upper portions; they are grouped round the star-shaped window of the 'coro alto' in front of which is a statue of the Virgin set on the terrestrial globe carried by St Francis. Inside, the retables which date from the second half of the eighteenth century stress the cult of the Madonna still further, as the high altar is dedicated to the Virgin of Ocotlán and the retables of the 'crucero' to the Virgin of Guadalupe and the Virgin of pity. The decoration of the octagonal 'camarín' was conceived by a theologian, Father Loiazaga, and executed by a Indian sculptor, Francisco Miguel (1713–23). The dome is an epitome of heaven. In the centre Pentecost is portrayed as the apparition of the Holy Spirit to the Virgin and Apostles. Round about are saints who are connected with her by their writings and their devotion: St Bonaventura, St Anselm, St Ildefonso, St John of Damascus, St Laurence Justiniani, St Peter Damien, St Bernard and St Thomas Aquinas. At the corners of the octagon are mirrors surmounted by angels. The lower part of the 'camarín' corresponds to the earth and is decorated with scenes from the life of the Virgin painted by Juan de Villalobos.

Perhaps the richest, and certainly the most remarkable from the iconographical point of view, of the retables in the cathedral at Mexico City is the 'altar of the kings' ('altar de los reyes') by Jerónimo Balbás, in the centre of the chevet. It does not receive its name from the sovereigns of Spain but from its main theme: a gathering of images of sovereigns who were also saints around the picture of the Adoration of the Magi. In other words, this is an Adoration of Magi chosen from the history of the Christian Church to succeed those of the New Testament. In the lower portion are grouped Queen Margaret of Scotland, the Empress Helena, Isabella of Hungary and Isabella of Portugal, the Empress Cunegund, and Princess Edith. Higher up are Hermengild, the Emperor Henry II, Edward of England, and Casimir of Poland, and, at the sides, Louis IX of France and Ferdinand of Castile.

The church of SS Prisca and Sebastián at Taxco was erected to the order of Don José de la Borda so that his son Manuel, who was a priest, could celebrate mass in a church built specially for him. Quite naturally, the Church whose minister the young man had become provided the basic iconographic theme, which was linked with the cult of the Virgin in her earthly life and in her apparitions at Tepeyac and the cult of the patrons of the building. Outside, the drops and fragments of vine at the feet of the columns surrounding the main door recall the blood of Christ on which the Church was founded. Baptism is represented by the Baptism of Christ set in the centre of the façade within a frame shaped like a shell, symbolising the grace of the sacrament; at the baptistery door, Faith, Hope, and Charity, lead to the pyx, the mystical body of Christ. Within, the main retable expounds the catholic conception of the Church. The foundations, in the lower portion, consist of the Twelve Apostles, the Four Evangelists, and the Popes. The Triumph of the Church, half-way up, is represented by the martyrs surrounding an Immaculate Conception and by the pre-eminence of Peter. At the summit the secret of the Church's strength is revealed by the vigilance of the Eternal Father. The theme of the Church is followed up in the other retables, some of which are noted here. In the retable dedicated to St Joseph, the saint is accompanied by John the Baptist, who also opens the way to the New Testament. The altar of St John Nepomuk represents the word of God received by the Church. The shells and pomegranates decorating this altar and that of the Virgin of the Pillar have an exact significance: the former, like that surrounding the Baptism of Christ on the façade, signify grace following on the acceptance of the divine message, the latter as they waste away scatter their seeds like the word of God. The paintings of the retable, the Immaculate Conception and the Virgin of Guadalupe in the 'crucero', the martyrdom of the patron saints of the church in the upper portions of the centre bay of the nave, and the scenes from the life of the Virgin in the sacristy, are all the work of Miguel Cabrera. Thus the Virgin is not only celebrated on several retables – there is also a fourth dedicated to Our Lady of Sorrows – but benefits from the talent of one of the greatest painters of New Spain. In the chapel of the Indians Cabrera also painted the Summoning of the Souls from Purgatory in the expectancy of Heaven – in other words, the Church in agony redeemed by the Church triumphant.

The church at Tepotzotlán provides an iconographic development on an even wider scale, the major subjects being the Jesuit saints and the adoration of the Virgin. On the façade, below the clerestory, stands the statue of the missionary St Francis Xavier, the patron of the church, naturally enough in a country rescued from paganism. At the sides are figures of St Ignatius, St Francesco Borgia, St Louis de Gonzague and St Stanislas Kotska. In the centre of the topmost storey is a sculptured group of the Virgin and Child. The Child appears again over the door holding the terrestrial globe. Thus, exaltation of the saints of the Order is followed by magnification of the Christian faith in a world dominated by the Virgin and her Son. Within, the main retable is dedicated, as of right, to St Francis Xavier, patron of the church; St Louis de Gonzague, St Stanislas Kotska, and St Ignatius also have their own altars. The Virgin is honoured twice – as Virgin of light and Virgin of Guadalupe; the retable dedicated to the latter includes a painting by Miguel Cabrera whom we have already noted at Taxco; he also portrayed the apparitions of the Virgin at Tepeyac on the vault of the 'crucero'. The Loreto Chapel answers to a cult which the Jesuits liked to propagate in Europe and America, and the dome of the 'camarín' behind displays the Descent of the Holy Spirit as at Taxco.

Ornamentation and types of decoration in Spain and Spanish America

Amid the confusion of orders typical of Baroque we have noted two features of such importance that they can be considered symptomatic of certain periods of its stylistic evolution: the Solomonic column and the 'estípite'.

In our scrutiny of those Spanish buildings that

Church of San Andrés, Madrid: decoration (after O. Schubert)

first employed Solomonic columns, we find that there are several variations of this feature, the best known being the Berninesque type: in one region, it could have been used at different dates in precious metals, retables and façades. Finally, it did not spread throughout Spain from a single native model, but was adapted from Italian prototypes. In Seville in 1595, the goldsmith Francisco Alfaro took Vignola as his model and used the Solomonic column in the Sagrario of the high altar of the cathedral; but this premature example was not immediately followed up. At the cathedral of Compostela the column was used for the first time in a baroque retable of 1625 in the Reliquary Chapel; it was carved by Bernardo Cabrera and has now disappeared. These columns were of the Hellenistic type similar to those of the Baldacchino of Old St Peter's which were probably known through the medium of engravings. This type was used again by Cabrera in several retables which no longer survive. On the other hand, the columns of the canopy projected by Vega y Verdugo for the high altar of Compostela cathedral (1658–75) was of the Berninesque variety; his undoubted aim was to rival the Baldacchino of St Peter's (1627–32), which was known to him. In Santiago he could also have studied the Solomonic columns portrayed in the tapestries given to the cathedral chapter by Philip IV in 1656, and he was also in touch with advanced circles in Madrid. There, Sebastián de Herrera Barnuevo used the column for his projected altar for the chapel of San Isidro in San Andrés, and Fray Juan Ricci who was both painter and architectural theorist included it in the illustrations to one of his treatises on painting written in 1659–62, but not published until 1930. In Galicia the use of the Solomonic column passed from retables and baldacchinos to façades; but it disappeared from them sooner than in other provinces. Nevertheless, it continued to play a primary part in 18th century altars as can be seen from the great retable in San Martín Pinario at Compostela by Fernando de Casa y Novoa (1738).

In Andalusia the earliest use of Solomonic columns was in the retables of the Jesuit church at Granada; these may be dated somewhere between 1630 and 1660 and were executed by Francisco Díaz de Rivero who was trained in Seville. On the other hand, the main retable, now destroyed, of the Cartuja at Jerez de la Frontera by José de Arce may be exactly dated to 1637. This same year saw the publication in Seville of the Jesuit Quintadueñas's book 'Santos de la Ciudad de Sevilla' which included a frontispiece decorated with four Berninesque columns; this type was subsequently used in retables at Seville including the background of the 'retablo mayor' in San Lorenzo by Francisco Dionisio de Ribas (1649–52), and also in architecture, though the Solomonic columns projected for the church of San Salvador by Bernardo Simón de Pineda were never realized. Leonardo de Figueroa made frequent use of this type of decorative support and it endured throughout the first quarter of the 18th century in competition with the 'estípite'.

Victor Manuel Villegas has traced the origins of the 'estípite' back to ancient Crete, and has pursued its development through Greek and Roman architecture, the art of Michelangelo, and Mannerism. Specimens may be found covering the entire 17th century in Spain, but they do not start to take on baroque characteristics before 1650–60. In Galicia there are some very early examples including the retable of the Reliquary Chapel of the cathedral at Compostela by Bernardo Cabrera (1625–30), and the tabernacle of the main retable in the church of the Colegio del Cardenal at Monforte de Lemos by Francisco Moure (1625–36); these, however, continued under the influence of Italian or northern Mannerism. The 'estípites' of the Portico Real de la Quintana at the cathedral of Compostela were not executed until the end of the century under the direction of Andrade, despite the fact that work was begun in 1658; they derive from Michelangelo via Serlio, but reflect influences from Madrid. There the 'estípite' seemed to acquire baroque characteristics more rapidly than in the rest of the country. On the second level of the cloister of Santo Tomás built by Donoso about 1655, and in the 'portada' of the Oñate Palace (1655–70), neither of which survive, the 'estípites' were still Mannerist, but heralded a fresh sculptural approach.

The contract for the main retable of the Merced Calzada, dated 1678, mentions 'estípites', but it is not possible to identify their style with any certainty. It is usually agreed that the first wholly baroque examples were those of the 'túmulo' designed for Queen Marie-Louise d'Orléans by José Benito Churriguera in 1689, as published by Vera Tasis y Villaroel. Churriguera used them again in the 'retablo mayor' of San Esteban at Salamanca, though in this case a major role is played by Solomonic columns (1693). The 'estípite' also formed a basic element of the art of Pedro de Ribera. In Andalusia its use expanded from the two main centres of Granada and Seville. Hurtado used it in his design for the altar of Santiago in Granada cathedral in 1707. It is easy to follow its development at Seville, extending from Mannerism to the first examples of Baroque, as indicated by the designs of the unknown architect D. Z., dated 1663, published by Antonio Sancho Corbacho.

Owing to its fragility the 'estípite' seemed reserved for use in wooden retables; yet it appears to have been employed first as a pilaster in buildings of stone or brick (Leonardo de Figueroa's façade of the Hospital de Venerables Sacerdotes in Seville, 1690). In these hard materials it was not used as a free-standing support before the mid-18th century. Jerónimo Balbás must have first introduced it as a free-standing feature in retables rather than incorporating it in the background, and examples may be found in his work prior to his departure for Mexico – in the cathedral at Seville and in the main retable of the Sagrario church completed in 1709 and destroyed through the lack of understanding of the neo-classicists. Other examples of his work are at San Juan, Marchena, in the choir stalls, and at San Lorenzo, Cadiz.

These two basic elements of decoration – the Solomonic column and the 'estípite' – sometimes competed with the ornamented niche, which increased in importance in Andalusia from the early 18th century onwards. They were also closely linked with many other motifs – volutes, scrollwork, rich foliage, and stars, which occupied a prominent position in the 'yeserías' of Southern Spain.

Façades were treated as if they were retables, so there was a close iconographical link between them, and it has also often been noted that the decoration of the latter to some extent echoed that of the former; nevertheless, their monumental impact remained impressive. The most noble and most original Spanish baroque façade is undoubtedly the Obradoiro of Compostela cathedral, built in front of the Romanesque pilgrimage church and Maestre Mateo's Pórtico de la Gloria. Its apparent unbroken unity nevertheless conceals the work of various architects. On the right hand side by the cloister is the bell tower, which had been begun by Peña de Toro and finished by Andrade. Casa y Novoa took advantage of the restriction imposed on him by this feature and erected a similar tower on the left; he marked the intervening space in front of the Pórtico de la Gloria which had to be preserved, heralded and lit, by a stone screen known significantly in Spanish as 'el espejo' (the mirror). A staircase with opposed flights built by Ginés Martínez after 1606 leads up to the platform from which the façade rises. The sweeping uplift of the towers is emphasized by the prominence of the pilasters; they correspond tier by tier and their impetus is not halted even by the balustrades, for they continue beyond them in small pyramidal shapes.

Faced by the main altar of San Esteban at Salamanca, the learned traveller Ponz only found it possible to admire Claudio Coello's painting of 'The stoning of St Stephen' in the upper portion. He was blind to José Benito de Churriguera's impressive conception. Above the lower tier that sets off the altar rise six lofty Solomonic columns covered with grapes and vine tendrils framing the baldacchino.

In the sacristy of the Cartuja at Granada, particles of faint white clouds seem to drift through the air, visual echoes of the walls. The architecture and decoration of this interior are of an unsurpassed virtuosity. The unequal bays unexpectedly induce a rhythmic advance towards the altar, which is skilfully lit from the dome set in front of it. The brilliance of marble, stucco, paint, and rare woods suggests an unreal world intended by its creators to captivate the senses of the monks and induce religious feeling. Narcisco Tomé's 'Transparente' in Toledo cathedral, earlier in date and smaller in scale, provides a similar effect.

Two lengthy building periods (1617–21 and 1645–54) were needed for the completion of the Pantheon in the Escorial, and the result was a natural combination of royal pomp and baroque richness. The tombs in the octagonal chamber are decked with bronze ornaments designed by Italian artists under the direction of Crescenzi, and with rich facings, the work of Alonso Carbonell.

Spanish motifs and types were developed in America, again resulting in a form of close-packed suspended decoration; but it was often rougher and more lavish, especially in official architecture. This succeeded in producing a magical type of atmosphere seldom found in the buildings of Spain. A survey of the spread of this decoration involves dividing it into categories as well as by regions. These categories may be roughly defined as based on careful imitation, fairly free adaptation and employment of an individual native style.

Quito kept up close artistic relations both with Spain and other European countries; this may be at least partially due to the spread of treatises and engravings, and the origins of the Jesuits who were sent to the city. Thus, in the Compañía, the influence of Brother Pozzo may be noted in the altars of the 'capilla mayor', and the 'crucero' attributed to Brother Georg Vinterer, who was born in the Tyrol in 1695 and sent to Quito in 1743 after a period in the mission of San Miguel at Omaguas da Marañon. The façade of the church, called 'purely European' by Diego Angulo Iñiguez, follows the scheme of the Gesù in its overall design; the architect is unknown, but may be placed in the school or circle of Andrea Pozzo. The Solomonic columns resemble those in the tapestry of 'The healing of the paralytic' after Raphael, and those of Bernini's Baldacchino in St Peter's. The sculpture, carved in grey stone from the quarries of Yúrac, was completed in two stages – from 1722 to

1725 by Father Leonhard Deubler and from 1760 to 1765 by Brother Venancio Gandolfi, a native of Mantua. The original design was strictly adhered to and the composition is remarkably unified.

Nevertheless, it was natural that distance from Madrid, social, religious and economic conditions, and the presence of a rich leisured creole population, should result in expressions of originality enabling art historians to define a second category of buildings. Thus, when Guerrero adopted one of Serlio's plans for the Pocito Chapel at Guadalupe, he gave it an individual touch by contrasting wall panels and the decoration of the upper levels. Above all, New Spain gave pride of place to the 'estípite'. Basically, the chronology of its appearance in Spain and America is of little importance. The essential factor is the impetus it was accorded in Mexico by two architects from Andalusia – Jerónimo Balbás, designer of the 'retablo de los Reyes' in the cathedral of Mexico City, and Lorenzo Rodríguez who pushed to its final limits the example provided by Hurtado in the altar of Santiago in Granada cathedral. Two of the three façades of the Sagrario of Mexico cathedral form a monumental rhythm of 'estípites' uniting in harmony the strength of the supports and the delicacy of the ornamental detail. The decorated niche, however, gradually began to compete with the 'estípite', equalled it in popularity, and finally won pride of place. This was a continous development: in the Sagrario of Mexico cathedral (1749–68) the 'estípite' reigns supreme; in the façade of Tepotzotlán (1760–62) the two features are equally balanced; in the entrance to the 'camarín' in the church of the Carmen at San Luis Potosí (c. 1770) and in the façade of the Valenciana (1765–88), the decorated niche has won the day. Perhaps the most representative example of the richly ornamented 'camaríns' and 'yeserías' of New Spain is the Rosary Chapel of Santo Domingo at Puebla.

Guatemalan architecture developed an individual type of decoration in conformity with its horizontal tendencies; striking examples of this may be found in the many ruined or restored buildings at Antigua.

There is a proliferation of small flat motifs set close together. On the façade of the church of the Carmen (1728) they even cover the columns of the upper storey, contributing, with the multiplicity and irregular projection of the pillars, to a forceful impression of the Baroque reminiscent, in the opinion of Antonio Bonet Correa, of the temples at Baalbek. These typical motifs may also be found in the exterior of the Merced (1656–90, 1767).

In Peru we find strong connections with Spanish art and sculptured retables, allowing a choice of available models and a variety of interpretations. The basic type of support is the Solomonic column, which passed from retables to façades about 1700. The plants depicted are those extant in America, but they do not always grow in the regions where the sculptors have represented them. At Cajamarca, the cathedral façade, dating from the first quarter of the 18th century, is a masterpiece of decorative sculpture; the powerfully accentuated ornament has been treated in depth and not merely as surface decoration. Cuzco suffered severely in the earthquake of 1659 and was rebuilt at a time when many recollections of the Renaissance and Mannerism survived. These, together with the art of the sculptors of retables, left their mark on the 'portada' of the cathedral (1651–57), the Compañía (1651–68), the cloister of the Merced (c. 1653–69) and San Sebastián (1664–78). The 17th century style continued without a break into the 18th century; a taste for traditional Renaissance rustication persisted. Nevertheless, the Solomonic column made its appearance: the unknown architect of the Sagrada Familia used a simplified form of the Berninesque type for the 'portada' (1723–35). At Lima, the rich decoration of the third quarter of the 17th century found full expression in the 'portada' of San Francisco whose sturdy towers make an impressive effect with their bands of rustication. The other typical 'portadas' at the Merced and, more particularly, at San Agustín (1720), date from the beginning of the 18th century; in the composition and decoration of the latter, the interplay of Solomonic columns and diffuse ornament produces an impression of richness, while the whole or broken pediments of

Potosí Cathedral: Baptistery door (after Iñiguez)

the central section which rise repeatedly above the level of the side storeys give an impression of invincible uplift. The Torre-Tagle Palace, completed in 1735, at first appears to be a lavish re-creation of the palaces of Seville with their oriental-style balconies and jalousies. In its luxury, however, it recalls the opulence of the viceregal capital and the fragmented broken pediments of the 'portada' repeat the usual rhythm adopted for the city's buildings.

The third category of decoration raises the difficult problem of the effect of the native population on design and also involves the possible survival of pre-Columbian themes. The feelings of the conquered peoples, deprived of their gods, their culture, and any control over the architectural conception of Christian churches, may have been transferred to the sphere of decoration. Such a transference is in agreement with a generally held theory. There are, in fact, certain buildings which appear more than an adaptation of European or Spanish designs. Treated in a flat compact manner in two-dimensional space, they give the appearance of having been recreated by the natives, who, in fact, provided the labour force and, quite frequently, the foremen. The great 'portada' of the cathedral of Zacatecas in Mexico is decorated with representations of the apostles in an arrangement of niches and columns expressive of a horror of the void, and constitutes one of the most magnificent examples of this trend. Compressed flat decoration reached its height in certain regions now forming part of Bolivia and Peru. It may be discovered at Arequipa on several buildings, the finest being the façade of the Compañía (1690); on the shores of Lake Titicaca, where it may be found on the 'portada' of San Pedro at Zepita, at the church of Santiago in Pomata, on the façade of Puno cathedral by Simón de Asto (1757); on the 'portada' of Santa Cruz de Jerusalém at Juli; on three doors of the façade of San Francisco at La Paz (1772–83) and at San Lorenzo, Potosí (1728–44). Some of these motifs have a strikingly pre-Columbian look. At the Compañía in Arequipa, there is a representation of a tiger-cat in the guise of the mythological beast that lived on an island in Lake Titicaca. Figures recalling pre-Conquest types may be found at Zepita on the 'portada' of San Pedro, and at Pomata on the altar of the 'sotocoro' of San Miguel. At Santiago in Pomata the motifs of the dome movingly re-create a native dance. Alfred Neumeyer, in his analysis of the art produced by the fusion of native and European elements, terms it 'mestizo'.

George Kubler, however, has shown that the existence of 'mestizo' art does not stand up to detailed analysis and that the survival of pre-Columbian forms and usages was very rare. He has proved that the features of pre-Columbian life which survived best were related to practical and administrative matters rather than artistic symbolism. From the technical point of view, it is wrong to see the continuation of the pre-Conquest spirit in flat two dimensional sculpture. This conception was also part of mudéjar art. More especially, it is the normal result of the oft-repeated translation of European motifs known only through the medium of engravings or drawings, both flat modes of representation. Certain motifs which seem to us typically pre-Columbian are often no more than recent revivals answering the needs of enlightened tourists; they have, therefore, no connection with the baroque period.

Every example should be examined individually. In this way it is possible to discover some definite borrowings from pre-Columbian symbolism, such as the insertion of obsidian as a symbol of the principle of life in 16th century crosses from the provinces of Michoacan and Hidalgo in Mexico. Some resemblances are particularly deceptive. The sun with a human face, carved on the church of Santiago at Pomata, has been incorrectly considered a pre-historic emblem; it is really Christian and an attribute of St Thomas Aquinas.

Decoration in Portugal and Brazil

Portuguese and Brazilian decoration appears completely different from that of the Spanish world, both in its aims and its outward manifestations.

In Portugal, baroque decoration did not flow from interiors to façades. Nor do the façades have the same elegance as those of Spanish churches. Their beauty lies either in a simple interplay of architectural features as at Os Grilos in Oporto, sometimes heightened by subtle motifs as in the church of the Third Order of Carmelites at Oporto, or in the contrast between surfaces painted in vivid colours and the frames of doors and windows with their varying degrees of ornament.

Vast areas in cloisters, chapels and palaces, are covered by 'azulejos'. A still more original feature in the interiors of churches is the carved, gilded, polychromed wood, known as 'talha'; this is used for altars and retables and sometimes spreads over walls and vaults. Its development is clearly later than Spanish Baroque; altars with baldacchinos did not appear in Portugal until the 18th century in the time of John V, while Seville already possessed an extremely fine example in the 'retablo mayor' of the church of the Caridad dating from 1670. This backwardness was accompanied by a host of unacknowledged debts: influences were transmitted from Spain to Portugal but hardly ever in the reverse direction. Centrepieces of Spanish retables frequently projected forwards, but in Portugal they were hollowed. Spanish decoration, at least in the 18th century, often tended to a predominance of structural motifs and to the dissolution of ornament; the 'talha', on the other hand, reveals a struggle for supremacy between ornament and architecture. Indeed, structure and decoration developed independently. The former changed more quickly than the latter but, in the late 17th century, both united to produce a monumental effect. However exuberant the decoration, a lasting taste for the 'talha' provided a foundation for a type of balance clearly revealing the influence of the Romanesque portal and a liking for the closed form associated with it.

The Baroque makes its first appearance in Portuguese retables shortly after 1650–60. The new form of art passed through the country from north to south and found its balance in the last quarter of the 17th century, transposing the conception of the Romanesque portal into the 'talha'. The resulting composition combined Solomonic columns, pilasters, archivolts with clear cut toruses, and a symbolic decoration of children, birds, vine-branches and grapes; the centre was reserved for the throne or tabernacle. Thus the altar appeared as a triumphal arch, plainer than if it had been built of marble, but far warmer in colouring. Two very fine examples of this type of 'talha' inspired by the Romanesque are the high altars of São Bento at Oporto, probably from the workshop of Antonio de Azevedo Fernandez and Domingo Nunes (c. 1704), and of Santa Clara-a-Nova at Coimbra of practically the same period.

Projected trompe-l'œil decoration for church at Barcelos, by Antonio José Landi, 18th century

Foreign artists, especially Italians, at the court of John V were responsible for a type of refinement most clearly expressed in sculptured ornaments and Solomonic columns. The latter are based on Bernini's and have spiral flutings on their lower portions; further up roses blossom in the hollow spirals. Niches adorned with curtains and surmounted by canopies add to the complexity of the design; the apex is no longer a closed tympanum but explodes in a world of angels, garlands, flames, and shells grouped round a central motif which may be heraldic, religious, or merely decorative. The 'talha' overflows over walls and vaults, forming a gilded niche in front of the altar.

The rococo 'talha' of the second half of the 18th century was typified by 'estípites', exuberant ornamentation, and a lack of formal balance; the decoration was no more than applied to the structure.

In Brazil in the second half of the 17th century and later, there was a spontaneous resumption of the contrast between a functional plan with relatively plain façades and lavish interior decoration of gilded wood, fake marble, and paintings. The monastery of São Bento at Rio is a typical example of such a contrast. The façade of the church–the frontispiece was completed in 1669 under the direction of Fray Bernardo–derives its simple beauty from the interplay of door and window frames and white surfaces. Within, however, the 'talha' reigns supreme.

Brazil's most original contribution to baroque decoration lies in the work of Aleijadinho in the province of Minas Geraes. He reveals his skill and simplicity as a decorator of façades by concentrating the ornament round doors and windows and at the apex, sharply defining the purity of the architectural lines. His earliest attempt was the remodelling of the frontispiece of the parish church at Moro Grande whose heavy ornamentation was related to the retables of the time of John V (1763). His early design for the façade of São Francisco at Ouro Preto, which is known from the project of 1766, stressed the door and the sculptured medallion of the vision of Alvernia towards the summit; the rococo ornamentation was added after the design was altered in 1774. The door of Nossa Senhora do Carmo at Sabará, designed in 1769, reveals for the first time the complete success of Aleijadinho's personal conception. Even if the design appears fragile, the skilful rococo rhythm absorbs the symbolic motifs of the crown, the roses and sunflowers, and Mount Carmel. In redesigning his father's project for the Carmo at Ouro Preto in 1770–71, he was able to make a harmonious distribution of walls, windows, and decoration. The door surround, the armorial bearings on their rococo cartouche supported by two angels, the oculus with its decorations, and the pediment surmounted by a cross, form an ascending central zone in which there is a balance between the openings and the rich sculptured ornament. On either side of the door are 'fragments of architrave curved inwards in the Chinese style and dominated by a shell motif' which Germain Bazin recognizes as the artist's personal signature. The design for the façade of São Francisco at São João d'El Rei (1774) is Aleijadinho's highest achievement in dealing with this type of front, which is richly ornamented, yet, at the same time, simple and poetic in feeling.

As 'entalhador' Aleijadinho made a similar contribution to the triumph of the rococo style which succeeded the Baroque of John V. It stressed more delicate connections between design, mass, and colour. Gold ceased to be predominant; white and other colours combined with it to form lively and delicate harmonies. By skilful detachment, statues gained in powerful effect, and the high altar appeared as a triumphal arch. Aleijadinho's basic contributions to this new style include the high altar of São José at Ouro Preto, designed in 1772, the scheme of decoration for the chapel of the fazenda of Jaguará near Sabará, executed c. 1780 (this has now been moved to the parish church of Nova Lima), the decoration of the 'capela mór' of São Francisco at Ouro Preto where the high altar, planned in 1778–79, was not completed until twelve years later, and the ornamentation of the nave of the Carmo at Sabará.

Plates

Madrid

147 Royal Palace, Plaza de Armas. The palace represents the work of two Italian architects. It was erected by Sacchetti (1738–1764) who altered the design of his master Juvara (1735–1736). In the background may be seen the centre of the south façade built by Sacchetti. To the west and east are two low galleries dating from the reign of Isabella II (1833–1868); the latter is visible in the photograph.

148–149 Plaza de Armas, south front. This section of the palace combines the varied sources of Spanish monarchical architecture. The ground-floor with its banded facings derives from Bernini's last project for the Louvre and from the garden front of Versailles.

150 Staircase. Charles III (1759–1788), on passing from the throne of Naples to that of Spain, entrusted the chief part in the designing of his palaces to the artists who had served him in Italy. Sabatini replaced the palace staircase with the one which exists today. His composition of parallel flights succeeding a single one is a majestic work, a worthy background to court life. It is, however, much less impressive than Sacchetti's design which consisted of two vast wells meeting in a great central hall on the upper floor.

Ecija

151 Palace of the Marquises of Peñaflor. The architecture of the patio reflects a noble simplicity: an Ionic order on the ground-floor, arcading above the upper floor windows, and ironwork balconies; the whole roofed with tiles.

152 Staircase well. The nobility of the patio is followed up in the triple arcading and increased by the added scale of the staircase and the richness of the 'yeserías'.

153 Staircase dome. Comparison of a dome of this type with examples from Spanish America reveals the strength of the link between them, despite original touches. The mudéjar tradition, so flourishing in Andalusia, developed in America and possibly fused with certain native tendencies quite ready to absorb it.

Lima

154 Torre-Tagle Palace (1735). Carved wood balcony. Balconies of this type (miradores), combining exterior and interior spaces, are a customary feature of Andean architecture, possibly originating in the Canary Islands. Their origin may also be connected with the far distant East.

155 Detail of the patio. Memories of Andalusia may be noted in the basic design and in the walls lined with azulejos.

156 Details of the patio.

157 General view of the patio. The balustrades, with their alternating long and short sections, repeat the rhythm of the upper galleries of certain cloisters in Lima. The arcades have been constructed with two different diameters; the smaller combine a trefoil arch with curved brackets; the larger, double curved brackets with re-entrant angles.

158 Detail of the patio. Azulejos played a considerable part in decoration in the Iberian peninsula and in Latin America – even more perhaps in the Luso-Brazilian world than in Spanish territories.

Antigua

159 Lateral façade of the University. As the 'portada' of the main façade dates from 1832, this view gives a better impression of the exterior aspect of the buildings after their completion in 1763. The blindingly white wall is pierced by polygonal windows alternating with the papal arms. The flat consoles imparting rhythm to this alternation include inverted S's typical of Guatemalan Baroque.

160 West gallery of the patio. The multilinear arches, the cushioned columns and consoles, striated surfaces, and massive pillars are all typical of Guatemalan Baroque.

161 Detail of the patio.

162 Detail of the patio. The gable of the gallery, surmounted by the papal arms.

Royal Palace of Madrid
Plan 1:1000

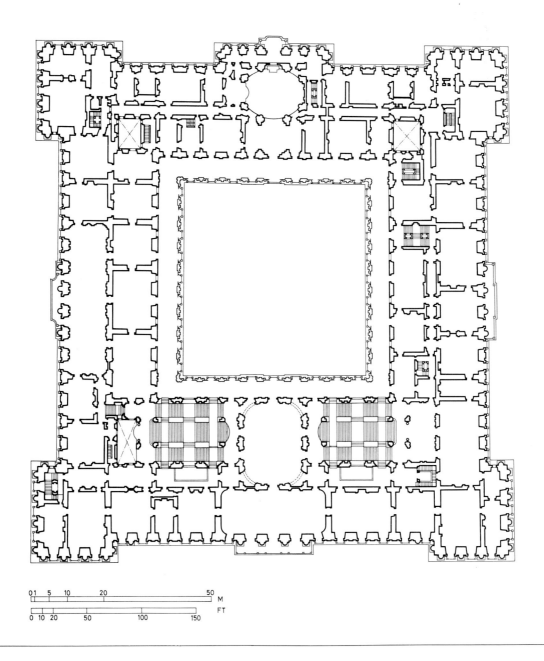

Torre-Tagle Palace, Lima (Peru)
Plan of the ground-floor and of the first floor 1:400

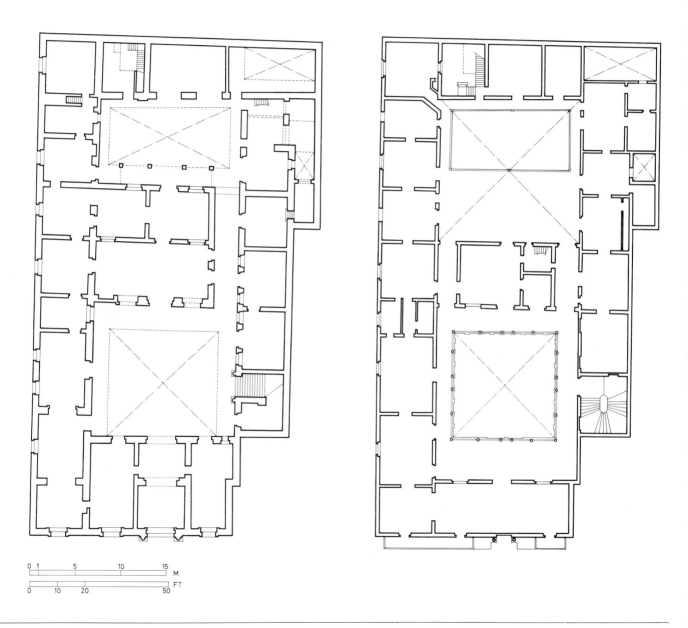

0 1   5   10   15
                        M
0   10   20   50
                       FT

Notes

Madrid

The Royal Palace. Madrid was artificially created capital of Spain and, for a long time, boasted no royal palace other than the former Moorish fortress standing on a steep slope overlooking the Manzanares; this building was embellished by Charles V, Philip II, and, more particularly, by Philip IV. It was burnt down during Christmas night, 1734, during the reign of Philip V, grandson of Louis XIV, and Isabel Farnese, a daughter of the ducal house of Parma. Both considered Spanish architecture too provincial compared with the styles of their native countries, so that the new palace, symbol and seat of the monarchy, was entrusted to an Italian. Juvara, a Sicilian in the service of the court of Turin, the leading contemporary Italian architect, heir to the tradition of Bernini and the Fontanas, was chosen a few days after the fire. He planned a royal residence on the scale of Versailles to be built on the heights of Leganitos, but died after he had been only a few months in Madrid. While court intrigue raged over the choice of a successor, Pedro de Ribera vainly drew up a grandiose plan typical of the Madrid style of Baroque. Finally, Sacchetti, a Piedmontese pupil of Juvara, was summoned to Madrid. The site of the ruined Alcázar was kept for the new palace, so Sacchetti altered Juvara's plan into a high building and erected the present palace into which the Court first moved in 1764. The most elegant and attractive of the interiors is the throne room with its Tiepolo ceiling – an allegorical composition depicting various facets of the Spanish monarchy (1764). The chapel is a sensitive rendering by Ventura Rodríguez of the Italian baroque style.

Ecija

Palace of the Marquises of Peñaflor. The palace presents a long front to the street with attractive painted decoration; at one end the door, several storeys high and richly decorated, bears the date 1726. The staircase beyond the patio is especially dignified and ornamented with 'yeserías'. This palace is one of the most typical of Ecija and the province of Andalusia on account of the contrast between the relative modesty of the façade and the scale of the buildings, the beauty of the courtyard and the amount of plaster decoration.

Lima

Torre-Tagle Palace. This palace was commissioned by Don José de Tagle y Bracho, paymaster-general of the Fleet of the Southern Seas, created Marqués de Torre-Tagle by Philip V; it was completed in 1735. The façade is notable for its lofty, sculptured doorway as monumental as a church 'portada', and for its carved wood 'miradores'. The upper storey of the patio develops into a rhythmic succession of large and small multilinear arches, each of which embodies a different decorative scheme. The palace is really a transposition of an Andalusian nobleman's house, but doorway, balcony and arcades are completely original touches. The building now houses Peru's Ministry of Foreign Affairs.

Antigua

University. The University of Guatemala, now Antigua, was founded in 1676 and was first housed in the former College of St Thomas Aquinas. The decision to transfer it to the site of the present buildings was not taken until 1753. According to Diego Angulo Iñiguez, it was designed by José Manuel Ramírez, member of a family of architects. Sidney D. Markman notes that, as it was a civil building, the surveyorship of the works devolved on the military engineer Luis Diéz Navarro who had come from Mexico in 1741 and had been commissioned to rebuild the palace of the Captains-General at Antigua; Markman also suggests that Navarro possibly drew up the plans. The building consists of a succession of rooms grouped round a vast patio. Its charm is basically derived from the multilinear arches of the galleries whose delicacy makes up for the massive strength of the pillars rendered necessary on account of the frequency of earthquakes. The buildings stood up to that of 1773 after which the city was abandoned and the present capital founded. The actual University was not transferred there until later, and a general restoration was undertaken in 1790. In 1832 a school was installed in the buildings, and the 'portada' of the main façade was set up in the same year. The rooms are now occupied by a Museum of Colonial Guatemalan Art. Set in the heart of the former capital of the kingdom of Guatemala, the University is one of the most elegant examples of the regional Baroque. Its walls and supports are solid, almost oppressive, but it attains a varied charm thanks to its superficial surface decoration and the delicate interplay of the arcades.

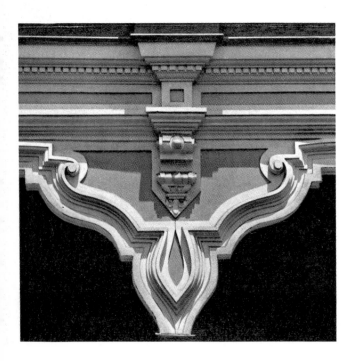

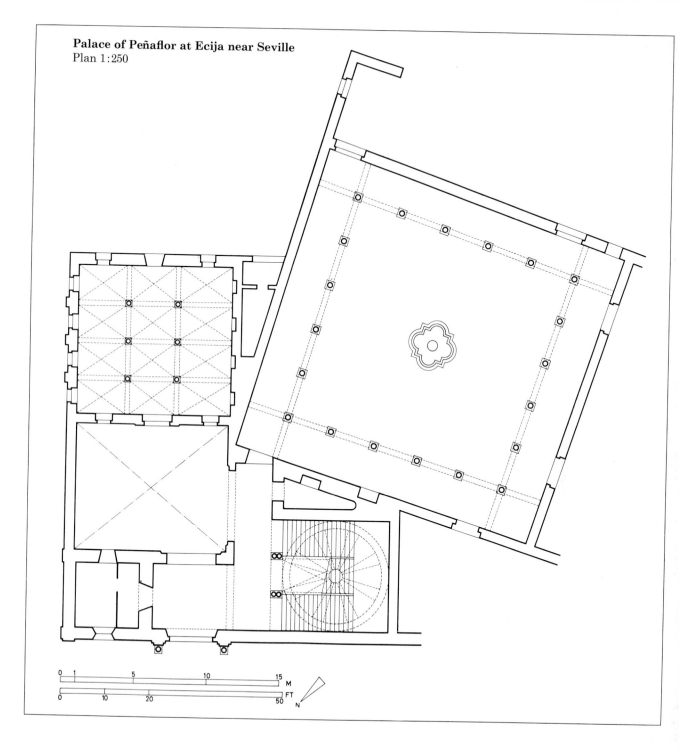

Palace of Peñaflor at Ecija near Seville
Plan 1:250

0 1   5   10   15 M

0   10   20   50 FT

N

San Carlos University, Antigua (Guatemala)
Plan 1:500, elevation and section of a portico 1:100

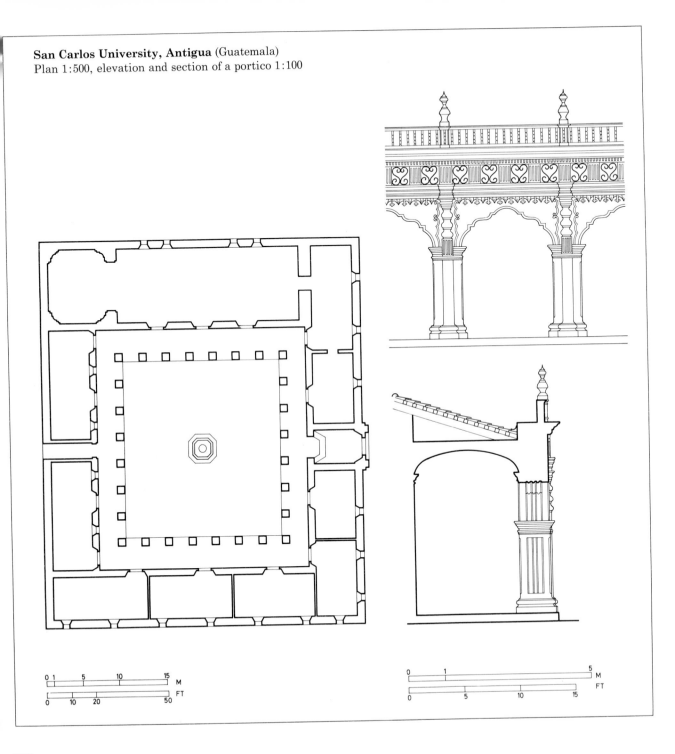

0 1   5   10   15   M

0   10   20   50   FT

0   1   5   M

0   5   10   15   FT

5. Town-Planning

Baroque town-planning –
French monarchical town-planning

Baroque town-planning may be defined by reference to characteristics identical with or at least similar to those of architecture; a study of one of the most notable examples, 17th and 18th century Rome, will make this clear. Historians and informed travellers will very soon discover the constant factors combining the effects desired by the builders: the element of surprise, desire for grandeur, and the part played by fountains.

Within the network of streets and squares outlined by Sixtus V (1585–90) and radiating from the pilgrimage churches, baroque Rome developed magnificently with the help of mathematical calculations and creative imagination. In the opinion of Pierre Charpentrat, Bernini's Colonnade in front of St Peter's should not be treated merely as an 'enclosure'; it constitutes 'an ambiguous architecture', 'the opposite of a wall' and must be considered as 'pure organization of space, the free realization of a town-planner's dream'. The Spanish Steps by A. Specchi and Francesco de Sanctis reconcile 'the ascent with the spatial expansion and pulsations of the Seicento city'. Nicola Salvi's Trevi Fountain with its square, gracefully indicates 'a type of town-planning based on surprise and the picturesque'. Palazzi are integrated with the city thanks to the emphasis of the 'piano nobile', the bold relief of their roofs, and their centralized façades; so are churches and fountains, which are also taken as key points in perspectives.

France, especially, in the time of Louis XIV and Louis XV, provided exceptional models quite apart from any stylistic criticism that may be levelled at them. This is not the place for a review of the respective roles played by Classicism and Baroque in French monarchical architecture. Careful examination indicates that Classicism was predominant in exteriors and façades, but that there were abundant traces of Baroque and Rococo in decoration and festival designs. It is important to note, however, how difficult it was for 18th-century sovereigns linked to the

French king by blood, marriage, or merely by a sense of admiration, to avoid being impressed, apart from all stylistic considerations, by the two most typical manifestations of Bourbon art – the palace and the 'place royale'. In France these were classical in style but elsewhere they lent themselves to transposition into Baroque. The palace, perfectly exemplified by Versailles, was not merely a princely residence and fit setting for the life of the sovereign, it was also the seat of government. It was situated outside the city and, by means of its park and gardens, gave the king and his court direct contact with nature. The 'place royale' – the Place des Victoires or the Place Vendôme for instance – linked the conception of a monumental piece of town-planning with respect due to the sovereign here represented by his statue.

The Hispanic conception of town-planning

The Spanish genius was to a great extent under Moslem and mudéjar influence and so preferred schemes based on interrupted axes set at right angles. Their designs favoured streets that cut back on themselves; they scorned limitless perspectives, preferring closed and subdivided spaces. Thus their buildings are not set off by squares or converging streets, but by their own twisting or ascending outlines.

Fernando Chueca Goitia has shown by careful analysis that the typical Spanish town remained up to the 16th century what he termed the 'convent-city' ('ciudad-convento'); its influence endured until the late 18th century in opposition to the 'palace-city' ('ciudad-palacio'), a Bourbon importation. In his own words: 'Many Spanish monasteries were founded directly after the Conquest in towns developed by the Moors. Though the churches were usually built to a new plan, the monastic buildings were enclosed within high walls which included houses, palaces and streets, forming huge, regular blocks of buildings which threatened to absorb the entire enclosure. The results of this usage passed from the realm of architecture to the wider one of the planning and shaping of our cities. These were developed under the influence of monasteries which imposed almost stifling restraints on the city's natural development. From this arose the typical Spanish city which may be termed the 'convent-city' as opposed to the 'palace-city' which the Bourbons attempted to introduce. This 'convent-city' is the town enclosed by walls, the inner city. The typically Spanish 'plaza mayor' is a product of the aesthetic conception of the monastery applied to town-planning. It is an individual case of an enclosed space originating from the cloister and answering the Moslem feeling for intimacy.

These basic tendencies of Hispanic town-planning raise a problem similar to that posed by architecture. By their feeling for surprise and the picturesque they result in Baroque. On the other hand, they are apparently in opposition to the open forms considered typical of the style by Wölfflin: they lack the desire for unity, dynamism, and perspective in depth, usually associated with it.

Thus we are left with a two-fold question to answer. Did a system of baroque town-planning exist in Spain? What, in fact, did the 18th century monarchs introduce into their kingdom?

Baroque town-planning in Spain

In purely Spanish town-planning, so very different from the Roman, the Baroque springs from the element of the unexpected and, still more, from the deployment of decoration. These two features are manifested in the seemingly haphazard plan of the streets of convent-cities, in the more rigid line of a right-angled plan, and in the unexpected revelation of a 'plaza mayor'. Great use is made of towers in conformity to a taste going back to Moslem and mudéjar art. Domes are not found so frequently, being opposed to national temperament, and are often covered with small caps. The richness of decorated surfaces is always achieved in accordance with certain geometrical laws and colour harmonies. The close-set relatively flat ornament restricted to well defined panels and the rectangular frames of doors and windows has already been considered in relation to individual buildings. Its lyric surge is really stressed in a town setting because of the contrast between the exuberant ornament and the restrictions imposed by the narrowness of streets, and the neighbouring houses. The word 'surge' is still more justified if it is extended to the decoration of domes and towers, which do not usually mark the end of a street or converging avenues but appear above a complex layout of roofs and walls that prevent one from seeing the base of the building until the very last moment. This flood of seemingly weightless, prismatic volumes and of surfaces which, by contrast, appear all the more intensively decorated, varies in tonality according to regions and individual towns, as has already been explained. It is subdued in Castile and, for the most part, in the north of the peninsula, but more highly coloured in Andalusia.

Civil buildings, particularly palaces, relied on 'portadas' to attract attention. A surviving example of this is the Hospicio de San Fernando at Madrid built by Pedro de Ribera. There was a similar feature at the palace in the Calle de Alcalá built by José Benito de Churriguera for his noble patron Juan de Goyeneche, treasurer to two queens, Mariana of Neuburg and Isabel Farnese, and ardent promoter of the manufacture of glass in Spain, as we shall see when we come to the building of Nuevo Baztán. The main door to his Madrid palace, now the seat of the Real Academia de San Fernando, was remodelled in the neo-classic style by Diego de Villanueva, but a drawing dated 1773 reveals its original state. The composition, with female figures in the angles and two children holding the central shell, formed one of the few vehement accents in a relatively sober façade. This building is a convincing if austere example, but the palace of the Marquises of Peñaflor at Ecija in Andalusia has more charm and atmosphere. The partly ruined interior boasts widely distributed, rich decoration. The columns of the patio are marble with jasper pedestals and cartouches. The staircase rises from the ground-floor in two parallel flights and continues with a second, single flight bridging the stairwell. This beautiful design is unfolded behind a long wall carefully following the curved line of the Calle Caballeros. One might almost suppose that the builders ignored this narrow street and turned their full attention to the interior. The truth is that they accepted the restrictions imposed by the design of the town and constructed a concave façade bordering the lane like a piece of theatre scenery. A wrought iron balcony supported by hooked consoles stresses the elongated curve of the wall; the lofty windows above are treated as motifs in a vast 'trompe-l'œil' painting. The eye glides over this curve of black metal and half sham, half real, architecture to come to rest on the profile, not the full face, of the main door (1726), its double portico (Ionic columns at ground-floor level, Solomonic columns for the 'piano nobile') and its coping (two heavy consoles from which a great multilinear arch seems to spring backwards). The splendid Peñaflor Palace clearly shows how a nobleman's house, while submitting to the outline of a town, radiates a note of elegance in the visual composition of its setting.

The Novitiate of the Jesuits at Seville, dedicated to San Luis, and their great college, the Clerecía, at Salamanca, furnish two very differing examples of religious houses in an urban setting. Both present their church in the same way: a high façade with two towers surging upwards from the edge of a narrow street. In Seville it is very difficult to get back far enough to judge the majestic beauty of the church of San Luis; the architectural composition can only be fully grasped if one stands a certain distance away to the side; a frontal view from the balcony of the houses opposite allows one to examine various decorative details, but does not permit an overall survey. At Salamanca the late 15th-century Casa de las Conchas stands across the narrow street from the Clerecía; from the patio of this house, one of the most noteworthy examples of Spanish late medieval domestic architecture, one may obtain the best view of the beautiful slender church towers with their rich decoration. As at Seville, a general view of the church can only be obtained from the side. Apart from this common characteristic, however, the two buildings are totally different. The Novitiate at Seville does not command attention; it stretches along the street behind a quite ordinary façade. The Clerecía, on the other hand, extends to either side of its church with lofty walls divided into geometrical compartments; this results in a powerful effect giving a confused impression of domination.

To explain the 'plaza mayor' as the transposition into terms of town-planning of a monastery cloister is insufficient. Its origins were also political – the development of municipal institutions by Ferdinand of Aragon and Isabella of Castile; commercial – to centralize shops and market halls after the fashion of Flanders and Northern Italy; and social – to construct a setting for the 'paseo', festivals, tournaments, public executions and 'autos-da-fé'. In addition there was the element of prestige, each city wishing to build a larger and more beautiful square than its neighbours.

The two 'plazas mayores' built in the 17th and 18th centuries at Madrid and Salamanca respectively comply with all these conditions.

The purchase of the ground for the building of the Plaza Mayor at Madrid began in 1581 when Juan de Herrera drew up a design for the square, but building did not start until 1617–19 in accordance with the plans of Juan Gómez de Mora. The restorations following the fires of 1672 and 1790 changed the original architecture, but the general arrangement and ground-plans were preserved. It is significant that the chief building, the Casa de la Panadería, served both as a shop for bread, as its name indicates, and as a box for the king and his suite on festival occasions.

The Plaza Mayor at Salamanca was designed by Alberto de Churriguera in 1728 and executed in accordance with his plans from 1729 onwards. The royal pavilion, completed in 1735, shows his remarkable talent for adapting Plateresque sources, so common in the town, to suit the vigour of the Baroque.

The Town Hall (1755) was erected after his departure by Andrés García de Quiñones, who chose a more grandiose style for the building. In deciding to build

Plaza Mayor, Madrid: detail from plan by Teixeira, 1656 (photo Bibliothèque nationale, Paris)

its own square, the city of Salamanca wished to create a more magnificent one than those of Cordoba ('El Cuadro'), Valladolid ('El Ochavo'), and even Madrid. This desire was fully achieved. The Plaza Mayor of Churriguera and García de Quiñones is one of the most typical works of Spanish Baroque, in which florid decoration is applied to a simple rectangular plan. It is also the most beautiful and most harmonious square in Spain by virtue of the pure simplicity of its design and its soft golden stone.

At Madrid, the Alcázar and its surroundings also accorded with the rules previously noted: a juxtaposition of disjointed buildings set round gardens and irregular courtyards, and a vast square with several narrow streets leading into it, overlooked by the main façade of the palace. The Alcázar was originally a Moorish fortress set on top of an abrupt slope rising from the valley of the Manzanares; it was transformed into a palace in the reigns of Charles V and Philip II. To the west it enjoyed a magnificent view over the Sierra de Guadarrama – one which Velázquez used as a background to some of his royal portraits. Philip IV embellished the exterior by commissioning

Alcázar and palace square, Madrid: detail from plan by Teixeira, 1656 (photo Bibliothèque nationale, Paris)

Juan Gómez de Mora to erect the monumental south front, which provided the palace square with a majestic background (1619–27).

The composition of the Alcázar of Madrid and its surroundings only partly concerns the baroque period. Nevertheless, before the building of the south front it served as inspiration for the palace and plaza of Lerma. The Duke of Lerma, favourite of Philip III, wished to receive the king in the centre of his possessions near Valladolid and to isolate their meeting-place from all outside influences. To this end he had a series of monasteries, houses and palaces, built in his ducal capital, which formed a notable example of Spanish town-planning, both from their unified conception and from the speed with which they were executed (1604–18). His architects were Francisco de Mora and Juan Gómez de Mora.

The 'ermitas' in the gardens at Lerma probably served as models for those at the palace of Buen Retiro at the eastern end of Madrid. This palace was typical of Spanish royal architecture in the 17th century. The development of the Alcázar was dictated by the original Moorish fortress and the hilly site, but for this completely new palace, Philip IV and his minister Olivares could have adopted a regular plan. This was not to be. There was a succession of courtyards without any general perspective, and no noticeable unity between gardens and buildings. Such at least is the impression given by engravings and plans showing the original state of this royal domain. Today all that remains is the present Army Museum, including the Hall of the Realms and the 'Casón' with its decorations by Luca Giordano. The 'ermitas' in the centre of their fretted basins probably constituted the most genuinely baroque features in the park.

Pedro de Ribera, under the patronage of the Marqués del Vadillo, crown governor of Madrid (1715–29), improved the appearance of the capital with fountains including the fountain of Fame, buildings of public interest, such as the Hospicio and the Toledo Bridge, and the park surrounding the Virgen del Puerto. These were only piecemeal improvements.

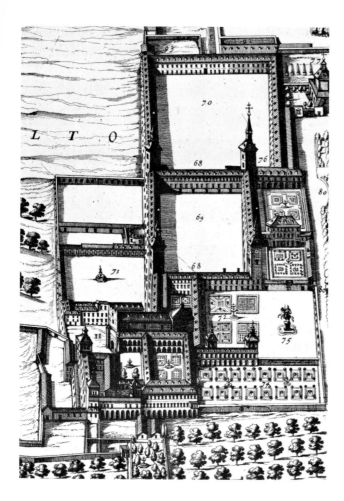

Palace of Buen Retiro, Madrid: detail from plan by Teixeira, 1656 (photo Bibliothèque nationale, Paris)

His unexecuted project (1736) for the completion of the Royal Palace shows, however, that he was capable of linking buildings with their environment. It is uncertain whether this project referred to the site of the destroyed Alcázar or, as its scale would appear to suggest, to that at Leganitos selected by Filippo Juvara for his own designs. At any rate, an admirable feature of this composition of five courtyards set in a cross is the way in which the same curved lines are repeated in the layout of gardens and buildings. It is

also noticeable that the parterres were not only to surround the palace but were to penetrate some of the courtyards and contrive to guide the eye towards distant perspectives. If this project had been realized, Spanish urban planning could have achieved a stateliness rivalling Italian Baroque.

At Nuevo Baztán, Goyeneche commissioned José Benito de Churriguera to build a glass manufactory, workmen's homes, a church, and a palace for the landowner. In this case, the architect adopted a square plan with discontinued axes at right angles to one another. The church is attached to the palace and their junction hides the plaza lying behind them. The layout of the town (1709–13) may be discovered by making a series of right-angled turns varied by some obvious diversions. The rigidity of the plan is offset by the austerity of the buildings, so that, once again, it is the decoration and the unexpected perspectives that provide the baroque effect.

At Santiago de Compostela this effect is induced by identical means coupled with the co-operation of the buildings. All round the cathedral are squares following the outlines of the medieval town; they vary in area and derive a picturesque note from their different levels, flights of steps, unexpected shapes, and the façades surrounding them. The Obradoiro faces the Rajoy Palace, started in 1766 in the classic style; on the other sides of the square are ranged the buildings of the Colegio de San Jerónimo with its 15th-century 'portada' and the Hospital Real (1501 to 1511); despite the different periods and styles of these buildings, the baroque façade of the cathedral above its flight of steps dominates the vast expanse of the square. On the Plazuela de las Platerías, opposite the Romanesque door of the cathedral, stands the Casa del Cabildo (1756). The bell tower and the baroque envelope of the chevet border the Plaza de la Quintería, from which an imposing flight of steps gives access to the Azabachería. This square stretches from the façade of the monastery of San Martín Pinario (1738) to the door of the cathedral transept, completed in 1770 after several remodellings extending from early Baroque to Neo-Classicism.

Monarchical planning in 18th century Spain

There are many aspects of this type of planning, so it is necessary to be selective. The restricted yet noteworthy efforts of the Marqués del Vadillo and Pedro de Ribera in Madrid, during the reign of Philip V, derived, as we have seen, from the native baroque style. The remodelling of the capital in the reign of Charles III was in the neo-classic manner exemplified by Sabatini's Puerta de Alcalá, and the layout of the Paseo del Prado by Ventura Rodríguez and the fountains of Cybele, Neptune, and the Seasons, designed to ornament it. The same reign saw the foundation of the settlement of La Carolina in the Sierra Morena; the town was built to a rectangular plan with the streets intersecting at right angles. There is noticeable attention paid to perspective, however, in the siting of the church and the large crossroads to the north. Apart from these examples, 18th century monarchical planning can be restricted to the layout of the royal residences – the relationship of the palaces to their ancillary buildings, gardens, and urban surroundings.

Its two main sources were the art of the Bourbons and that of the Italians, with a marked tendency to transform into the Baroque alien features borrowed from French monarchical culture.

During his marriage to María Luisa of Savoy, Philip V came under the influence of her chief lady-in-waiting, Madame des Ursins; he first of all entrusted the task of transforming Buen Retiro into a palace in the tradition of Versailles to French artists. In 1712–14, Robert de Cotte from Paris drew up four plans which, with varying degrees of success, attempted to transform this part of Madrid in the French manner. On the whole he respected the buildings constructed under Philip IV, linking them to a palace, whose approach avenues, courtyards, and reworked gardens were typical of the style of Louis XIV.

After the death of María Luisa of Savoy, the king married Isabel Farnese; at Jadraca on 23rd December 1714, even before meeting her husband, she dismissed Madame des Ursins so that she might have sole control over the king's mind. In spite of his youth passed in France, the king wished to rediscover in Spain the gardens rather than the palaces of his childhood, those of Marly in preference to those of Versailles. The king and queen agreed to support a court art of Franco-Italian origin, strengthening the prestige of the throne; compared to this the Madrid Baroque of Pedro de Ribera appeared provincial and reactionary. Isabel Farnese employed Italian architects, but gardens, fountains, and sculptures, were inspired by French influence.

The estate of La Granja is a typical example of this type of division. The nerve-racked king wished to abdicate and had a palace designed for him by the architect Teodoro Ardemáns in the mountains near Segovia; this palace was a miniature Alcázar with four corner towers and a Colegiata chapel in the centre of the west front (1721–23). The beauty of the estate derived less from this building than from the gardens, which were those of Marly transposed into a mountainous site. A few months after his abdication, the king was obliged to remount the throne as the result of the death of his son Luis I (1724), but La Granja remained his favourite residence. The Italian architects Procaccini, Juvara, and Sacchetti, remodelled the palace in accordance with their native style and the gardens were considerably enlarged.

After passing through the gates from the Segovia road, one is faced by a narrow area between the service wings; this subsequently widens and leads up to the Colegiata and the royal apartments of the palace. This arrangement cannot, for several reasons, be compared to the courtyards of Versailles which become increasingly narrower, culminating in the Cour de Marbre. At La Granja the area leading up to the palace is a large garden that widens instead of narrowing; it does not end at the sovereign's bedchamber but at the Colegiata, which occupies the centre of the buildings after the pattern of the Escorial. The curved centre of the church façade and the lateral bell towers corresponding to those of the original castle give this section of the palace a striking resemblance to certain baroque buildings of Central Europe. Indeed we are here faced with a coincidence and a possible case of imitation. Ardemáns' 'Alcázar' originally had four towers but these were reduced to two by Sacchetti, who removed those at the north-west and south-west corners as they destroyed the harmony of the new buildings facing the park. As for the Colegiata façade, the central curve and the two bell-towers in front of Ardemáns' church are additions dating from the time of Procaccini (1729–34), possibly modelled on an engraving by Fischer von Erlach. On the garden side, both the main east front and the courtyard to the south are in the Italian style. The gardens are French both in their layout and by virtue of the sculptures, especially those by René Frémin and Jean Thierry; but there are basic differences to the garden designs at Versailles and Marly. Here the palace lies at the bottom of a slope, trees grow right up to the wings of the east front, and the ground is divided into a series of parallel perspectives brought about by successive purchases of land. Water from the neighbouring sierra gushes forth more abundantly than in the royal residences of France and a feeling for the picturesque redolent of the styles of the Régence and the Rococo replaces the serene grandeur of the art of Louis XIV.

The Alcázar at Madrid was destroyed by fire on Christmas night 1734. Philip V and Isabel Farnese immediately decided to rebuild the palace. On 31st December, Philip's minister Patino reported to the Spanish ambassador in Turin that the king wished to summon 'the Sicilian architect who designed the cathedral at Lisbon; we do not know his name but he is in the service of the King of Sardinia'. This was, in fact, Filippo Juvara, who had been responsible for the façade of the Palazzo Madama and the Superga at Turin and had also designed the luxurious hunting palace of Stupinigi outside the city. He arrived in Madrid in April 1735, and drew up a grandiose plan to be carried out on a site at Leganitos. After his early death in January 1736 he was replaced by one of his Piedmontese pupils, Sacchetti. To fall

in with the wishes of Philip V, who wanted to keep the palace as the seat of the monarchy on the original site of the Alcázar, he had to modify his master's plan by turning a building which should have been extended to maximum length into a high one. His palace was inspired by Bernini's second project for the Louvre rather than by Versailles and especially concerned the urban development of the hilly slope to the west of Madrid on which it stood. This development raised thorny problems owing to the need for providing a forecourt to the south and of linking the palace to the gardens on the east and west despite the violent shifts in the level of the ground. The proposed methods of solution were sought either in the gardens of Versailles which do not take account of the sudden changes of level, or in the spirit of Italian Baroque. In fact, none of the projects of Sacchetti and his contemporaries were ever realized.

In 1742, Étienne II Boutelou, by birth a Frenchman but later master-gardener at Aranjuez and La Granja, presented a plan for the gardens: to the north they were comparatively restricted but, at the foot of the palace to the west, they formed a vast, somewhat monotonous, composition of arbours and parterres. In Paris in 1746, Garnier d'Isle, 'surveyor general of buildings, arts and manufactures to His Majesty' (Louis XV) proposed an extended garden on the north side and, below the palace, a vast parterre set between groves in groups of four on each side.

None of these designs, despite their fidelity to the tradition of Lenôtre, showed the poetic imagination and mingled charm and dignity evinced by Ventura Rodríguez when he conceived a plan for the surroundings of the Royal Palace (1759). Taking his inspiration from Roman Baroque and especially from Bernini, he devised a circular garden-square and made up for the differences in level by ramps and steps radiating round a central temple set on a platform with fretted corners.

The old palace of Aranjuez, which had been planned by Juan de Herrera for Philip II, was considerably enlarged by Philip V to designs by Pedro Caro Idrogo dated 1715. After being burnt in 1748 in the reign of Ferdinand VI, it was rebuilt by the Italian architect Santiago Bonavia with the grand staircase and main façade that still reflect the personality of this careful royal architect. In 1750, the old town was levelled and rebuilt by Bonavia with the assistance of Alejandro González Velásquez and the French architect Jaime Marquet. The wings facing the 'Plaza de Armas' to either side of the main façade were by Sabatini (1771–81), but the three architects just named were responsible for the dignified, skilful layout of the town adjoining the gardens of Philip IV and Philip V and centred on the palace and the chapel of San Antonio. These two buildings are linked by arcaded galleries to the Casa de Oficios. The architecture of the chapel imposes its curved lines on the section of the square to which it forms a background: in front of the rear rectangular and centre elliptical chambers, a third, circular in plan, imparts its wavy lines to the portico and galleries that radiate from it. Thus Bonavia appears as a baroque town-planner capable of designing a vast palace and a church with complex volumes as major motifs in many-sided perspectives.

Fountain of Neptune, in the palace gardens of Aranjuez (photo Bibliothèque nationale, Paris)

Town-planning in Spanish America

From the very beginning of the Conquest, the Spaniards made conscious efforts to introduce urban development, which eventually advanced despite earthquakes and the ruins resulting from them. Their coherently planned cities were far in advance of those built by the English and French in their American possessions. In his account dating from the second half of the 17th century (1666–97), François Correal gives an admiring description of Lima: 'The streets are beautiful and perfectly straight, but the houses have only one storey, seldom two, because of the earthquake. Moreover, they are beautiful (at least those which are near the Plaza), their fronts ornamented with long galleries... Trees have been planted round the houses to protect them from the heat of the sun. They regain in width and depth what they have lost in height'. Then, under the influence of his memories of Europe, he devotes a few lines to the Plaza Real which he finds 'very beautiful. In the centre is a bronze fountain ornamented with a figure of Fame which projects a jet of water. The east and west sides are lined by various fine, well-designed public buildings'.

The Spaniards did not introduce that complicated product of several centuries of Spanish and Moslem history, the plan of the 'convent-city', to the New World. For complex reasons, frequently debated by historians of town-planning and outside the scope of this book, both conquerors and conquered adopted a checkerboard layout with a central plaza and streets intersecting at right angles. As has been noted, François Correal referred to the streets of Lima as being 'perfectly straight', and Fray Francisco de Ajofrín expressed admiration for those of Mexico City 'which intersect with the greatest regularity from east to west and north to south, forming perfect right-angled crossings'.

Nevertheless, these square plans differ from their

European counterparts in individual characteristics. The founders and builders of the American cities conceived them on a vaster scale as space was not denied them; obviously, too, the wish to dazzle the natives with monumental splendour also played a part. The result of this desire was a clarity and legibility of plan that is immediately obvious to a visitor from Europe. There also followed a characteristic less easy to define: American cities turn outwards more than Spanish ones. The feeling of intimacy from which the latter derive so much charm is discarded in favour of spaciousness.

How do baroque values fit into this urban layout? The effect of surprise usually found in Spain is often done away with, or at least weakened, in America because of the spaciousness of the squares and the regularity of the streets. It is replaced, however, by an emphasis on dignity. Cathedrals and churches with many towers and domes rise from an uncluttered urban horizon so that it is possible to admire their silhouettes and decoration from many viewpoints. The ornamented façades of palaces, convents, and sanctuaries, throng rectilinear streets. Thus, the checkerboard plan, basically so stiff and dry, becomes a support for monumental dignity and decorative exuberance.

Some individual towns may be noted within this general survey.

Antigua in Guatemala is formed of square blocks of streets surrounding a central plaza. This is bordered by the Ayuntamiento (Town Hall), the cathedral, with a wide rich façade, and the palace of the captains-general, whose most striking features are a noble regular portico at ground-floor level and a gallery above; the strongest baroque note is struck by the pediment of the central section. The plaza was paved in 1704 and in 1738 the centre was ornamented with the fountain which still stands there; the present garden, on the other hand, is a 20th century creation. The general impression, despite the lavish ornament of the cathedral, is one of official dignity. The atmosphere gradually shifts, however, in favour of deco-rative richness as one sets out to explore the wide streets of Antigua and discovers motifs peculiar to the façades of palaces and, more frequently, of churches. The gates of the University and the 'Colegio Tridentino' face the side entrance of the cathedral with a square between them. This small square is one of several adorning the city; in fact, the town plan included a dozen or so minor squares, which increased the decorative effect. The expanse of space and sky revealed by these squares does not avoid a certain aridity, caused by the rigidity of the overall town plan. A note of charm additional to richness of decoration is offered by the fountains, which unite physical freshness to the continuously repeated music of their waters.

Sorely tried by frequent earthquakes and capital of an agricultural region, Antigua could not rival the elegant cities of New Spain. It is on these that we must now concentrate.

In his analysis of their history and sources in the Acts of the 20th International Congress of the History of Art, Joseph Armstrong Baird Jr reaches a definition previously stated in this book: Baroque results from the effect produced by individual buildings and from the sum of these effects, but not from any overall conception. 'In Mexico after 1600,' he writes, 'there was comparatively little of the carefully conceived spaces before individual buildings, or of the elaborate inter-relation of scale and mass, in terms of streets and the "piazze" or "places" of a metropolis, which were developing in baroque Rome and Paris. The result is that Mexican architecture often consisted, after the 16th century, of isolated buildings related in a physical, but rarely in a cohesively planned manner, to their metropolitan, town, or country sites'.

Morelia has a notable ensemble of monumental buildings set within the traditional checkerboard plan. There are many towers, including those of San Agustín, San José, and the cathedral. The latter stands in the centre of the town, clear of other buildings, with squares to right and left of the main façade. The interior is basically 17th century, but the façade, the feature which probably proves most striking to the spectator and gives character to the face of the town, bears the date 1744; in accordance with traditional composition, two towers frame the dignified dome lying further back. The Seminary, built by Bishop Sánchez de Tagle (1757–72) and now occupied by the Governmental Palace, harmonizes to some extent with the richness of the neighbouring cathedral but appears somewhat lower in comparison. Two of the churches – Santa Rosa with a 'portada' of 1757 and Las Monjas – line the streets with their sumptuous wall decoration. With regard to Morelia, however, baroque town-planning should only be mentioned with extreme care. The relative sobriety of the style distinguishes the city from Mexico City and Puebla and stresses the severity of the checkerboard plan. In the opinion of Joseph Armstrong Baird Jr the emphasis placed on the cathedral constitutes 'a special case of baroque scale with double Renaissance spaces partially planned in the 19th century'.

He also makes a similar statement regarding Mexico City. As we might expect, in the capital city of New Spain, buildings such as churches, convents, colleges, and palaces, were very richly decorated but continued to be considered as isolated units. A pre-Hispanic plan was used for the rebuilding of the town after the Conquest and was usually respected later on. An exception may perhaps be made regarding the cathedral square, now generally called the Zócalo. It is bordered by the cathedral, its Sagrario, and the Palace of the Viceroys. The equestrian statue of Charles IV by the neo-classical sculptor Tolsá that now stands on the Avenida de la Reforma was destined for this square. There was, however, no real attempt to remodel this fine site in accordance with the design provided by Bernini for St Peter's Square in Rome. As for the few radiating streets to be found in the city, they are late 19th or 20th century additions. In the immediate neighbourhood of the capital the general tendency of Mexican town-planning is upheld by Guadalupe. The basilica, the Pocito chapel and the Cerrito chapel on the hill of Tepeyac where the Virgin made her appearance do not form a coher-

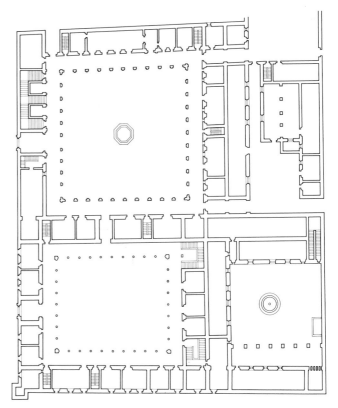

Palace of the Viceroys, Mexico City, 1709: plan

ent ensemble. The ramp up to the latter chapel is a picturesque form of road, as may be seen from a drawing in the Archives; it does not really constitute an attempt to unite separate buildings scattered over undulating ground. The esplanade now stretching in front of the basilica is an entirely recent creation. This inability to connect organically features related by function and the lie of the land contrasts with the remarkable coherence of the pilgrimage sites of Portugal and Brazil.

The Mexican genius was especially skilful at conceiving isolated buildings and could handle the bold insertion of churches into the middle of the countryside. This is demonstrated by the sanctuary at Ocotlán where the atrium serves both as a square and a means of transition to the immense sweep of the landscape.

175

The Jesuit reductions

The typical plan of the reductions is easily definable. The whole mission, built to an orthogonal plan, was designed round a great square plaza. To the rear of this plaza, forming the extremity of the main axis of the settlement, stood the church, between the cemetery and the college or residence of the Jesuits. Near this residence were shops and workshops and behind the chevet of the church were gardens. The remainder of the plaza was bordered by the Indians' houses, which spread over the major part of the reduction along the rectilinear streets. Near the college was situated the 'cabildo', the municipal building of the natives, and the 'cotiguazu', an establishment reserved for widows. Further off was the 'tambo' or inn. In some missions there were individual touches such as an octagonal plaza with four small chapels; the part played by these was similar to that of the 'capillas posas', which, in 16th century Mexico, were used for processional halts at each corner of the courtyards of churches and convents.

The functional logical plan of the reductions was based on the right angle and allowed the number of native houses to increase without any difficulty. It did not, however, especially derive from Baroque. This style was, in fact, capable of development in the sphere of church decoration.

Town-planning in Portugal and Brazil

Luso-Brazilian temperament manifested its capacity for spatial organization in pilgrimage sanctuaries, the layout of the gardens and palace of Queluz, and the rebuilding of Lisbon.

In the case of pilgrimages we must recognize the cult of Calvary, which was assisted by the erection of 'sacred hills'; these included two masterpieces – the Bom Jesus do Monte near Braga in Portugal, and the Bom Jesus de Matozinhos at Congonhas do Campo in Minas Geraes, Brazil.

Mountains reaching to the heavens were already considered intermediaries between men and divinities in the pagan world. They received their final consecration and real meaning from the death of Christ, whose blood flowed over the skull of the first man entombed at the foot of the Cross. This belief is only the general frame for the Christian thoughts that must serve to guide us round the Bom Jesus at Braga.

The Crucifixion formed the object of a cult on the Monte Espinho near Braga before the baroque period since, at the beginning of the 14th century, it was occupied by a hermitage dedicated to the Holy Cross. The brotherhood of the Bom Jesus do Monte, founded in 1629, restored the chapel, saw to the construction of approach roads, and had chapels built for the 'pasos'. Their efforts lent a new impetus to the pilgrimage which had fallen into decline. The dean of the chapter of Braga who had been responsible for this took renewed interest in the Bom Jesus when it had again become a source of profit, and evicted the brotherhood. In 1722, however, the brothers, with the backing of the bishop, Dom Rodrigo de Moura Telles, asserted that the dean was once more endangering the pilgrimage after taking over its direction, and got him to renounce his rights. Dom Rodrigo became the 'juiz' of the brotherhood and undertook a vast architectural and iconographic programme on the sacred hill, probably entrusting its execution to the colonel of engineers, Manuel Pinto de Vilalobos. The work was begun in 1723 and consisted of the entrance portico, the chapels of the 'Via Crucis', a section of the staircase of the Five Senses, and several fountains. A second building period about 1740–50 resulted in the fountain of Saturn and another section of the staircase. The fountains of Jupiter and the Five Wounds of Christ, and the pedestals of the statues in the centre of the staircase date from a third building period after 1774. The neo-classic architect Cruz Amarante was commissioned to rebuild the church which was falling into ruin. Before starting this, he executed a detailed model of the entire pilgrimage area; the new church was begun in 1784. The 19th century saw the building of the staircase dedicated to the Theological Virtues, the replacement of six of the eight chapels of the 'Via

Crucis' and some minor modifications. Thus it is important for the visitor to the Bom Jesus to separate the iconographic, topographical and architectural programme of the baroque period from the present appearance of the building.

The entrance portico has survived, with the keystone emblazoned with the arms of the bishop, Dom Rodrigo. On either side are two fountains carrying the emblems of the sun and moon. Germain Bazin in his detailed analysis of the setting and meaning of the pilgrimage writes of the two heavenly bodies: 'Near the Cross they signify the violent transition from day to night which followed on the death of Christ; the sun which floodlights truth is the New Law and the moon which is merely its reflection, the Old Law'. They also possess 'a link with the conducting of souls to the dead' and, in a wider sense, 'express the eternity of the world'. Beyond the portico the 'Via Sacra' rises up the mountain in zigzags passing the chapels, only two of which now date from the 18th century; these chapels house the 'pasos' from the Last Supper to the Crucifixion. The pilgrim then reaches a landing where the rococo fountain of the Five Wounds of Christ receives water from the staircase of the Five Senses; the water flows through serpentine channels recalling the brazen serpent, precursor of the Cross.

The architectural, but not the iconographical, prototype of the staircase of the Five Senses is that of the Benedictine monastery of Tibaes. In accordance with tradition the fathers attached a humanist interpretation to the staircase, combining Christian and mythological motifs. The statues were not changed but the pagan allusions were transformed.

We next reach the staircase of the Theological Virtues (1837) and the new church built by Cruz Amarante. In the baroque era, one first came to a labyrinthine garden dating from 1732–45. This constituted a 'symbol of the world in its complexity striving towards unity' and also 'the best representation of the condition of man, the adventurous pilgrim on this earth'. The church was completed in 1725 to an elliptical plan resembling as closely as possible that of the Holy Sepulchre. On the summit of the mountain are two chapels. One, dating from the time of Dom Rodrigo, houses the 'paso' of the Deposition from the Cross, the other, built in the 1750s, the 'paso' of the Resurrection. The staircase leading up to them was decorated in the 18th century with statues of Joseph of Arimathaea, Nicodemus, the Centurion, and Pilate. These now stand in front of the church together with the reconstructed statues dedicated to the four judges of Christ.

Before the reforms of the late 18th century, the Bom Jesus do Monte represented unity of place, thought, and art. It constituted a real 'microcosm, designed round the Redemption, the pole of world history'.

We may rediscover the same conception at the Bom Jesus de Matozinhos, created by the genius of the sculptor Aleijadinho.

In the province of Minas Geraes where mines were the source of wealth, Feliciano Mendes, a diamond prospector, fell seriously ill and vowed to devote his life to the cult of an image of Christ or the Virgin. In 1758, he opened the alms register of the sanctuary he had founded the year before, modelled on the Bom Jesus de Matozinhos near Oporto; this sanctuary was centred on a cross and a chapel at Congonhas do Campo. This Brazilian Bom Jesus achieved great fame despite the death of its founder in 1765. In fact, it was not modelled on the one at Oporto, but on the Bom Jesus at Braga. The church was completed about 1771 and, about ten years later, work began on turning the neighbouring hill into a 'sacro monte' similar to the one at Braga. The 'pasos' of the chapels on the 'Via Crucis' and the prophets for the church terrace were commissioned from Aleijadinho and his workshop; the former date from 1796–99, the latter from 1800–5.

The 'Via Crucis', constructed over the mountainous terrain, links the six chapels of the 'pasos' which were not built until 1802–18. The pupils and assistants of Aleijadinho played a great part in the execution of the sculptures but the statues of Christ reveal the master's hand. After the Chapel of the Last Supper, there follow those of the Mount of Olives, the Taking of Christ, the Flagellation, the Crowning with Thorns, the Carrying of the Cross, and the Crucifixion.

Next one reaches the terrace of the church set amid the vast landscape and outlined against the sky, both of which contribute to the beauty of the sanctuary. A semicircular 'perron' leads to the first two flights, which rise directly facing one another; two other similarly opposed flights help to complete the ascent. Statues of the prophets designed to recall the truth of the Incarnation combine in a kind of sacred ballet whose movements only seem uncoordinated; once these sculptures cease to be considered as isolated units, they take on full signifi-

cance as part of a huge composition brought to life by an inspired genius. Directly by the stairs stand Isaiah, Jeremiah, Baruch, Ezekiel, David, Hosea, Jonas, and Joel, with Amos, Nahum, Obadiah, and Habakkuk, at the fretted corners of the terrace.

The Bom Jesus at Congonhas do Campo is simpler than its prototype at Braga and respects the basic design of the 'sacro monte' with regard to an iconographic programme and use of space. Moreover, it possesses an inestimable treasure in Aleijadinho's sculpture – an evocative power far superior to that of its model.

The 'sacro monte' represents utilization of space for religious ends. The palace of Queluz, on the other hand, may be regarded as a secular example designed for court use. It must, however, be stressed that it was not a royal domain in the strict sense of the phrase, but the residence of a royal prince. Under the Braganza dynasty, up till the revolt of Dom Miguel, it belonged to the Infantado and was, to some extent, the apanage of the reigning sovereign's younger brother.

During the first building period from 1747 to 1752, Mateus Vicente de Oliveira erected the ceremonial north façade and the two wings framing it in a U-shaped curve. These buildings, facing the future site of the garden of Neptune, were destined for the Court; the unpretentious elegance of their façades contrasts

Hill of Calvary, Congonhas do Campo, Brazil: plan

1 Chapel of the Last Supper
2 Chapel of the Mount of Olives
3 Chapel of Taking Christ
4 Chapel of the Flagellation and the Crowning with of
  Thorns
5 Chapel of the Carrying of the Cross
6 Chapel of the Crucifixion
7 Terrace of the Prophets
8 Church of the Bom Jesus do Matozinhos

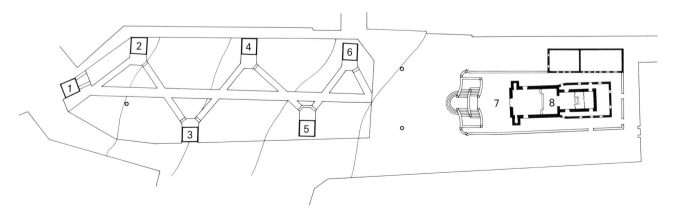

with the relative meanness of the office buildings on the entrance side. When Oliveira was summoned to the rebuilding of Lisbon after the earthquake of 1755, the work at Queluz devolved upon Robillion, who started his activities in 1758. Behind the west wing of the ceremonial façade he adapted the slope of the ground to a building on two levels; one corresponded to Oliveira's work, the other, below, was preceded by a colonnade supporting a terrace. This generally admired composition was completed in 1779. José Augusto Franca, however, criticizes it for its lack of unity: the lower storey appears to him 'in the style of Mansart', inspired by the Orangery at Versailles, while the upper one is in a 'highly impure' Louis XV style – a hard judgement, which does not take the lyrical beauty of the place into full consideration. Robillion also planned the gardens. The garden of Neptune lies in front of the ceremonial façade (1758) that faces the gate of Fame leading into the park. This gate is decorated with two winged horses copied from the pair at the Reservoir of Marly by Coysevox, ridden by Fame and Mercury. The garden of Malta faces the east wing, while the Jamor river, canalized since 1755, flows into an elongated basin embellished with azulejos.

At the time that Queluz was being developed, the rebuilding of Lisbon gave Pombál and the city merchants an opportunity to realize an undertaking of even greater scope (by virtue of its artistic, political and social significance).

About 9.40 a.m. on Saturday 1st November 1755, Lisbon was ravaged by an earthquake whose successive shocks lasted for nine minutes; these were accompanied by emissions of sulphurous vapours, tidal waves on the Tagus, and a fire that was to last six days. The Court was in residence at Bélem and escaped unscathed from the disaster. Joseph I, seized with terror, henceforward chose to live in wooden cabins and placed his confidence in the statesman whose great capacities had been revealed by the catastrophe – Sebastian Joseph de Carvalho e Melo to become famous under the name of Marqués de Pombál. The minister ordered the military engineer

Manuel de Maia to rebuild the capital, paying special attention to the Baixa or lower town; Maia was already an old man – he was born in 1677 – but he was to be assisted by Captain Eugenio dos Santos and Carlos Mardel. The plan for the Baixa was strictly geometrical with streets at right angles stretching between the Rocio and the Praça do Commercio; the latter lies to the south and is bordered by the Tagus. The sober aspect of the houses gives this network of streets a premature neo-classic look; this did not arise from a deliberate adoption of style but resulted from desire for uniformity and functional necessity. As has been frequently noted, the checkerboard or grid plan can become baroque through abundance of decoration. This abundance is lacking, however, in Pombál's Lisbon.

It is difficult to see Pombál's Lisbon as a finished example of the town-planning of the Enlightenment; Portugal had only limited contact with the Europe of the Philosophes and Manuel de Maia himself regretted the lack of books that prevented his studying the great examples of architecture of his period. On the other hand, the rebuilding of the city was undoubtedly the work of Pombál and the bourgeoisie who supported him. Though the sovereign's statue ornaments the Praça do Commercio, the royal palace has completely vanished. The new Lisbon is not so much a city based on a certain style as the creation of a certain social class and a great minister.

To sum up, town-planning in the Iberian and Ibero-American worlds found its most convincing expression in royal residences, a field especially open to foreign influences, and in façades – that is to say, once more in the sphere of decoration.

Conclusion

As the historical background and the buildings of the period have been gradually defined in the various chapters of this book, the problems raised in the introduction have been answered in accordance with actual circumstances and the most likely hypotheses. To conclude, we should briefly return to these problems and their solutions with a view to making a synthesis and, if possible, to go beyond this.

Perhaps it may be questioned whether a form of Spanish baroque architecture ever really existed. Those who remain strict devotees of the definitions of Heinrich Wölfflin, which were remarkable for their time, will be tempted to deny its existence. Of course Wölfflin in his 'Kunstgeschichtliche Grundbegriffe' based his inquiry on Italy and Germany; Spain to a great extent escaped his established norms. The only strict deviations from them are a limited number of buildings and the royal residences built in the 18th century. Subsequent to the succession of the Bourbons the latter constituted a formal statement of European monarchical art in which French, Italian and German influences were united in a comparatively restrained form of Baroque; this type of Baroque made use both of rich interior decoration and a skilled handling of space. There is, however, very little development of the latter in buildings, especially churches, in the authentic Spanish tradition apart from the invention of the 'camarín' and the customary use of the 'sagrario' as display case for the 'transparente'; the merit of these buildings is almost entirely due to their decoration.

Submission to a common, often authentic distinction, the obligations imposed by the customary plan of the 'Living Architecture' series and the need for a clear progressive argument, have resulted in structure and ornament being treated separately. In conclusion, however, it is all important to reunite features that have been separated in the previous chapters. Decoration is an integral part of Spanish baroque architecture. Such a statement, however, is too much of a simplification when applied to actual buildings and the conception of town-planning. Generally speaking, it is dangerous to divide buildings into summary categories: those which are based on the conception of volumes, those which form a close union of mass and decoration, and those which are virtually pure decoration. Let us, therefore, examine the commonest tendencies of Spanish baroque architecture. It appears that little or no attention was paid to walls, supports, and roofs, from the spatial angle; there was an overruling tendency towards well defined plans and prismatic volumes, and, within these, a forceful use of ornament emphasized its dominance. Light, which is so important in baroque effects, plays amid the ornament that is to some extent substituted for the architectural envelope to form a number of interior spaces. Thus the double function of the decoration is revealed: it plays its natural part and also helps to create shifting lyrical spaces that throw into the background the static well-defined spaces of the structure. Indeed, the structure sometimes seems to have been designed merely to permit the expansion of the ornament.

Such a conception is clearly far removed from that to which we have become accustomed in France and Italy, where space is articulated between walls and roofs. The individuality of Spanish architecture so brilliantly maintained throughout the 17th and 18th centuries may possibly be explained by the geographical factor of the country's enclosure by mountains but, more probably, by Moslem influence and the requirements of the form of Christian worship practised by the Spaniards. Seeking to stress its originality throughout the long period ending in Neo-Classicism, Fernando Chueca Goitia has proposed the term 'mudéjar-baroque' ('barrocco-mudéjar'); this recalls the long tradition of building and town-planning in which decoration was firmly embedded; in this period, as in the past, it continued to be close-set, suspended, and relatively flat.

Among the problems set by the architecture of Spanish America, its relation to the Baroque and the nature of the latter are closely connected with the solutions that have just been propounded for Spain. As in the mother country, preoccupation with space is only revealed in a few selected buildings and the basic emphasis of the constructions and their connection with the Baroque are defined by their decoration. The variation of opinion echoed in the introduction has been confirmed, especially through the agency of the 36th Congreso Internacional de Americanistas held at Seville in 1966. Gasparini stated here that in his opinion Spanish-American architecture could not be baroque because it lacked a feeling for space. Diego Angulo Iñiguez forcefully repeated his insistence on the decorative character of Spanish-American Baroque, and Antonio Bonet Correa made the following statement: 'The problem of space does not only exist in plain interiors; a new feeling for space is produced in decorated interiors. This exists in a whole series of variations. A space is created which is different from the one in which we move defined by the position of the walls. It is another type of space.' These observations link up exactly with those we have just made and the case may now be considered proven: architecture cannot always be reduced to a structural performance and historians are entitled to consider that of the Hispanic world baroque on account of its decoration, which is not only ornamental richness but a force capable of creating new spaces.

The argument just put forward presupposes recognition from the outset of a certain dependence in Spanish America on the mother country. But this dependence does not indicate uniformity.

This dependence on the mother country puts the originality of regional arts to the test. The problem is made complex by emotional considerations. Desires, whether conscious or not, to avenge the Indian peoples conquered by the Spaniards or to glorify the unity henceforward acquired by the descendants of both sides have led to strange results, even in art history. Some scholars, noted for the interest of their unpublished research, their intuition, and discernment, have let themselves be carried away: they must support the survival of the Indian temperament beneath the outward show of the viceroyalties, thus linking pre-Columbian art with that of the nations which achieved independence after their emancipation in the 19th century and proving the fusion of pre-Columbian culture with that imported from Europe. According to them this tendency is perhaps most violently revealed in Mexico, where it is the admitted truth that baroque architecture, a thoroughly national art, results from the close union of native, creole, and Spanish sources, and Indian and Hispanic feeling.

This is an attractive theory, for it is simple, allows the conquered to be reconciled with their conquerors, and ensures that a modern nation may grasp the sum total of its cultural heritage. The question is whether it is possible to subscribe to this synthesis. In the first place it should be noted that it is somewhat dangerous to consider the art of a period of dependence as the expression of future nationalism. Then, as has already been stated in this book, the vast expanse of building and decoration in Spanish America does not constitute a uniform ensemble. It is necessary to distinguish different strengths of imitation and originality. Some buildings are pure European importations. Others can be ranked as regional adaptations of an architecture stemming from the mother country and recalling the arts of the pre-Columbian period in tone or by certain decorative features. Beyond all doubt, in the baroque period, the new force of creole society, enriched and sure of itself, was transformed into architecture and its expression may be contemplated in some extraordinary buildings, especially in Mexico. Similarly, it is certain that the survival of Indian motifs is very rarely found in the baroque period. Two problems remain to be solved: on the one hand there is a clear resemblance between baroque and native themes, notably round Lake Titicaca, on the other the fusion of Hispanic, creole and Indian feelings. With regard to the former George Kubler's observations on the provincial repetition of motifs known through painting or engraving, both flat methods of reproduction, carry great weight; they can only be refuted by reliance on a conviction based on faith in the survival of the native genius rather than on reasoned argument. It is in accordance with this faith that one either accepts or refuses the fusion of Spanish, creole, and Indian feeling. Perhaps Hispanic Baroque developed its overseas exuberance in an automatic, physical way like certain imported plants; or perhaps the union of cultures and genius was responsible. The buildings offer clear evidence of exuberant decoration but, in our view, do not enforce either of these explanations.

Is the coherent, varied ensemble of the architecture of Spain and Spanish America especially connected with that of the Luso-Brazilian world? In both cases the buildings are almost all religious and sculptured wood or ceramic decoration is a prominent feature; in Portugal and Brazil, however, these three elements are probably more accentuated. Where stylistic evolution is concerned, Spain appears to have a lead over Portugal, who owes a considerable debt to her neighbour. On the other hand, a taste for the partitioning of space in churches seems to be common to both Hispanic and Luso-Brazilian architecture. This resemblance does not stand up to close examination, however. In the Hispanic world this division was engineered after the completion of a building designed conventionally with nave, aisles, transept, and ambulatory chapels; it was brought about by purely decorative features such as retables, grilles, 'sillerías', and screens for the 'sagrario' and 'coro' ('trassagrario', 'trascoro'). In Portugal and Brazil, on the other hand, partitioning formed part of the original interior design of a compact building – the national character favoured a type of 'parish church city', 'incorporating all the annexes to the sanctuary in a unitary plan', to quote Germain Bazin.

This preference is an indication of the profound originality of Luso-Brazilian architecture, which constitutes a whole chapter of Iberian and Ibero-American architecture and not merely a variation on Hispanic architecture. There are numerous proofs of its individuality in the period with which we are concerned. The success of the 'sacro monte' has no equivalent in the Spanish world.

How is the architecture of Brazil related to that of Portugal? It prolongs into the 17th century the experiments and duality noted in the various regions of the mother country; in this period it is possible to speak of unity on both sides of the Atlantic. During the following century, however, local variations appeared in Brazil and the architecture of Minas Geraes may especially be considered as a rococo blossoming of formulae that had already been elaborated in Portugal.

This brief attempt at a synthesis must also admit its limitations. The relationship of Iberian and Ibero-American baroque architecture to that of Italy and monarchical France is beginning to be fairly well understood, but this cannot be said of the links attaching it to Central European Baroque. Apart from some individual cases such as the arrival of the Jesuits in the regions concerned, we are usually reduced to noting resemblances without knowing whether these arise from coincidence, influence, or affinity. On the other hand, when we are able to see Iberian and Ibero-American architecture as more than a formal repertory – in fact, as the expression of a society and a period of catholicism – we may be able to fathom the entire scope of the religious phenomenon which it interprets; for this architecture shows what a large variety of peoples believed to be the doctrinal teaching resulting from the Council of Trent. Comparisons should be made with architectural styles in medieval Europe, particularly Romanesque, which it closely resembles from the artistic point of view in the extraordinary proliferation of forms.

It is a vain hope that this present age will ponder over every aspect of this lesson. At least, the basic catholic message has remained the same after the relegation of so many episodes in the lives of Christ, the Virgin and the saints, to the store of the religious picturesque, along with all the piety that nevertheless enabled quite a few souls to achieve nobility. Another lesson of the architecture we have just studied is, however, within the grasp of everyone. This is the lesson of forms, though it does not concern us here to determine exactly what assistance these can provide today. Everyone knows, however, that some of the greatest contemporary architects have been born or are working in the Iberian and Ibero-American worlds, for example in Brasilia. Thus we may make one sure affirmation: the amazing synthesis of knowledge, poetry, and profusion, represented by Iberian and Ibero-American baroque architecture is capable of inspiring the creators of the future.

Chronological Table

Historical Background

1581 Philip II, King of Spain since 1556, becomes King of Portugal
1598–1621 Philip III
1621–65 Philip IV
1624–54 The Dutch masters of part of Brazil
1628 Matanzas
1640 Revolt of Catalonia and Portugal; the latter proclaims the Duke of Braganza king under the name of John (João) IV (1640–56)
1643 Death of Louis XIII. Accession of Louis XIV. Rocroi
1659 Treaty of the Pyrenees
1665–1700 Charles II, King of Spain
1668 Spain recognizes the independence of Portugal
1683–1706 Pedro II, King of Portugal
1700 Spain passes to the Bourbons; the Duc d'Anjou becomes Philip V (1700–46)
1703 Treaty between England and Portugal brought about by Lord Methuen
1706–50 John V, King of Portugal
1746–59 Ferdinand VI, King of Spain
1750–77 Joseph I, King of Portugal; ministry of Pombál
1755 Lisbon earthquake
1756–63 Seven Years War
1759 Expulsion of the Jesuits by Pombál
1769–88 Charles III, King of Spain
1767 Expulsion of the Jesuits from Spain and Spanish America
1807 (27–29th November) The Portuguese royal family sails for Brazil
1808 (5–6 May) Meetings at Bayonne resulting in Napoleon I's attempt to make his brother Joseph King of Spain

Spanish and Spanish American Baroque

1604–18 Lerma, by Francisco de Mora and Juan Gómez de Mora

c. 1605–89 Quito, church of the Compañía

1614 Salamanca, Clerecía, by Juan Gómez de Mora

1617–19 Madrid, Plaza Mayor, y Juan Gómez de Mora

1628 Toledo, Jesuit church and Madrid, San Isidro, by Francisco Bautista

1633 Madrid, Buen Retiro, by Alonso Carbonell

1642 Madrid, chapel of San Isidro in the church of San Andrés, by Pedro de la Torre

1647–67 Valencia, chapel of the Virgen de los Desamparados, by Diego Martínez Ponce de Urrana

1650–90 Puebla, Rosario Chapel of Santo Domingo

1651–57 Cuzco, main portal of the Cathedral (by Francisco Domínguez de Chaves y Arellano?)

1651–58 Cuzco, church of the Compañía, façade by Juan Bautista Egidiano

1657 onwards Oaxaca, interior decoration of Santo Domingo

1657–73 Lima, San Francisco, by Constantino de Vasconcelos

1667 Granada, design for the cathedral façade by Alonso Cano

1680 Saragossa, design for the Pilar by Herrera the younger

1681 Loyola, project by Carlo Fontana

1683 Saragossa, tower of the Seo, by Contini

c. 1688 Mexico City, cloister of the Merced

1690 onwards Córdoba (Argentina), cathedral

1695–1709 Mexico City, Guadalupe basilica, by Pedro de Arrieta

1698 Arequipa, Compañía

1699–1731 Seville, San Luis (by Leonardo de Figueroa?)

1701–07 Valencia, main portal of the cathedral, by Conrad Rudolf

1702–20 Granada, sacristy of the Cartuja, by Francisco Hurtado

1704 onwards Granada, sacristy of the cathedral, after Francisco Hurtado

1709–13 Nuevo Baztán, by José Benito de Churriguera

1718 onwards El Paular, sacristy of the Cartuja, by Francisco Hurtado

1718 Madrid, hermitage of the Virgen del Puerto, by Pedro de Ribera

1720 Lima, façade of San Agustín

1721–23 La Granja, palace by Ardemáns

1721–32 Toledo, Transparente in the cathedral, by Narciso Tomé

1722 onwards Madrid, Hospicio de San Fernando, by Pedro de Ribera

1722–29 Cadiz, start of work on design for the cathedral, by Vicente Acero y Arebo

1724 onwards Seville, San Telmo, by Leonardo de Figueroa

1722–25 and 1760–65 Quito, façade of the Compañía

1724–31 Oaxaca, Rosario Chapel of Santo Domingo

1728 Antigua, Guatemala, Carmen

1728 onwards Salamanca, Plaza Mayor, by Alberto de Churriguera; completed by Andrés Garcia de Quinoñes

1735–64 Madrid, Royal Palace, by Sacchetti after a design by Juvara

1735–49 Murcia, cathedral façade, by Jaime Bort

1735 Lima, Torre-Tagle Palace

1738–49 Santiago de Compostela, Cathedral, Obradoiro, by Fernando de Casas y Novoa

1749–53 Madrid, San Marcos, by Ventura Rodríguez

1750–55 Salamanca, Clerecía, towers and cloister by Andrés García de Quinoñes

1751–59 Taxco, Santa Prisca, by Diego Durán

1760–62 Tepotzotlán, church façade

1771–91 Mexico, Guadalupe, Pocito Chapel, by Guerrero y Torres

c. 1780 Guanajuato, Valenciana

1790 Puebla, Casa de Alfeñique

Portuguese and Brazilian Baroque

1582 Lisbon, São Vicente de Fora, by Filippo Terzi

1598 Coimbra, church of the Jesuit College

1614–22 Oporto, Os Grilos, by Baltasar Álvares

1649–96 Coimbra, Santa-Clara-a-Nova (by João Turriano?)

1652–53 Lisbon, Santa Maria Divina Providência, by Guarino Guarini

1657–72 São Salvador (Brazil), church of the Jesuit College

1657–80 Oporto, Congregados

1673–87 Evora, Espirito Santo

1679–82 Elvas, church of São Salvador

1682 Lisbon, design for Santa Engracia, by João Antunes

1686 Oporto, São Victor

1691 Braga, Franciscanos

1715–44 Mafra, University Library, by J. F. Ludovice and Claude de Laprade

1716–46 Evora, choir of the cathedral, by J. F. Ludovice

1717 Work started on the palace-monastery of Mafra, by J. F. Ludovice

1723 to C 19 Bom Jesus shrine, Braga

1732–54 Oporto, church and tower of São Pedro dos Clérigos, by Niccolò Nasoni

1747–67 Queluz, by Mateus Vicente de Oliveira, Robillion, and an unknown Portuguese architect

c. 1748 onwards Mariana (Brazil), São Pedro dos Clérigos

1750–61 Lamego, Nossa Senhora dos Remedios; C 19 staircases

1753–85 Ouro Preto (Brazil), Nossa Senhora do Rosario, by António Pereira de Sousa Calheiros

1758 Lisbon, approval of plans for the Baixa. The city to be rebuilt by Eugenio dos Santos and Carlos Mardel, under the direction of Manuel de Maia

c. 1758–c. 1776 Congonhas (Brazil), church and terrace

1766–94 Ouro Preto (Brazil), São Francisco de Asis, by Aleijadinho

1770–95 Ouro Preto (Brazil), Nossa Senhora do Carmo, by Aleijadinho

1775 (6 June) Lisbon, inauguration of Machado de Castro's equestrian statue of Joseph I on the Terreiro do Paço

1796–1805 Congonhas do Campo (Brazil), statues on the staircase and terrace by Aleijadinho

References to Italian and German Baroque

1625 Baldacchino in St Peter's, Rome, by Bernini

1630 Venice, S Maria della Salute, by Longhena

1638–67 Rome, S Carlo alle Quattro Fontane, by Borromini

1642 Rome, S Ivo alla Sapienza, by Borromini

1656 Rome, Cattedra of St Peter, by Bernini

1657 Rome, Colonnade of St Peter's, by Bernini

1667 Turin, Chapel of the Holy Shroud, by Guarini

1668 Turin, S Lorenzo, by Guarini

1700 Vienna, Belvedere Palace, by Hildebrandt

1702 Melk, start of building works by Prandtauer. Prague, St Nicholas, Mala Strana, by Dientzenhofer

1711 Dresden, Zwinger, by Pöppelmann

1714 Vienna, Karlskirche, by Fischer von Erlach

1720 Würzburg, start of work on the Residenz, by Neumann

1722 Dresden, Frauenkirche, by Bähr

1728 Rome, Spanish Steps, by A. Specchi and F. de Sanctis

1729 Stupinigi, by Juvara

1732 Rome, Trevi Fountain, by N. Salvi

1734 Munich, Amalienburg, by Cuvilliés

1735 Rome, façade of St John Lateran, by Galilei

1752–74 Caserta, by Vanvitelli

Glossary

Adobe	Dried earth shaped like bricks, used in building construction
Ayuntamiento	Town hall
Azulejo	Square tile
Camarín	Chapel housing an especially venerated statue or relic
Capilla mayor	Main chapel of a church, housing the high altar, occupies the position of the choir in French cathedrals
Coro	Canons' or monks' choir, including the stalls ('sillería'); the 'coro' usually occupies the portion of the nave after the transept crossing and is surrounded by a space known as the 'trascoro'. In some churches or chapels belonging to religious orders the 'coro' is situated above the entrance and is thus called 'coro alto'
Crucero	Transept crossing
Cúpula encamonada	False dome mounted in a wooden armature
Enfoscado	Rough-cast
Estípite	Type of pilaster tapering towards the base; with the Solomonic column used in varying forms in Baroque architecture
Imafronte	Central section of a façade, between the towers. Subject of magnificent decoration in Mexico
Portada	Decorative work round the doorway of a religious or secular building
Presbiterio	Space near the altar, sanctuary
Retablo mayor	Main reredos of the church, retable of the 'capilla mayor'
Sagrario	Chapel housing the Holy Sacrament
Sillería	Range of stalls within the 'coro'
Tezontle	Volcanic stone (Spanish America)
Transparente	Great tabernacle forming an architectural feature within the Sagrario as in El Paular, Granada. Can also take the form of a retable as in Toledo cathedral
Trasaltar	Space round the 'capilla mayor'
Trascoro	Space round the 'coro'
Trassagrario	Section of ambulatory behind the 'altar mayor' (altar of the 'capilla mayor')
Túmulo	Catafalque used for funeral services (honras)

In Portuguese 'capela-mór' is the equivalent of the Spanish 'capilla mayor'; 'talha' indicates carved, gilded, and polychrome wood.

Bibliography

General works

Charpentrat, P.
Le mirage baroque. Paris, 1967

Charpentrat, P.
L'art baroque. Paris, 1968

D'Ors, E.
Del barocco. Madrid, 1931

Minguet, P.
Esthétique du Rococo. Paris, 1966

Tapié, V.-L.
Baroque et Classicisme. Paris, 1957

Tapié, V.-L.
Le Baroque. Paris, 1961

Wölfflin, H.
Renaissance und Barock. Munich, 1888

Wölfflin, H.
Kunstgeschichtliche Grundbegriffe. Munich, 1915

Monographs

Angulo Iñiguez, D. and others
Historia del Arte hispano-americano. 1950–1956

Bazin, G.
L'architecture religieuse baroque au Brésil.
Paris, 1956–1958

Bazin, G.
Aleijadinho et la sculpture baroque au Brésil. Paris, 1963

Bottineau, Y.
L'art de Cour dans l'Espagne de Philippe V, 1700–1746.
Bordeaux, 1962

Braudel, P.
La Méditerranée et le monde méditerranéen à l'époque de
Philippe II. Paris, 1949

Buschiazzo, J.
Historia de la arquitectura colonial en Iberoamérica.
Buenos Aires, 1961

Carvalho, A. de
D. João V e a arte do seu tempo. Lisbon, 1962

Cervera Vera, L.
El conjunto palacial de la villa de Lerma. Valencia, 1967

Chaunu, P.
L'Amérique et les Amériques. Paris, 1964

Chueca Goitia, F.
Invariantes castizos de la arquitectura española.
Madrid, 1947

Dos Santos, R.
L'art portugais. Paris, 1953

Dos Santos, R. and others
Historia de Arte em Portugal. Oporto, 1942–1953

Fernández, J.
El retablo de los Reyes. Mexico, 1959

França, J.A.
Une ville des Lumières. La Lisbonne de Pombal.
Paris, 1965

Giedion, S.
Space, time and architecture. Cambridge (Mass.), 1959

Hagen, O.
Patterns and principles of Spanish Art. 1943

Hamilton, E.J.
War and prices in Spain (1651–1800). Cambridge (Mass.),
1947

Kelemen, P.
Baroque and Rococo in Latin America. New York, 1961

Kubler, G. and Soria, M.
Art and architecture in Spain and Portugal and their American dominions 1500 to 1800. London, 1959

Kubler, G.
Arquitectura de las siglos XVII y XVIII. Madrid, 1957

Kubler, G.
On the colonial extinction of the motifs of Pre-columbian art. Cambridge (Mass.), 1961

Lavedan, P.
Histoire de l'urbanisme. Paris, 1942–1949

Lozoya, Marqués de
Historia del Arte hispánico. Barcelona, 1945

Mâle, E.
L'art religieux de la fin des XVIe, XVIIe et XVIIIe siècle. Paris, 1952

Markman, S.D.
Colonial architecture of Antigua Guatemala. Philadelphia, 1966

Mauro, F.
Le Portugal et l'Atlantique au XVIIe siècle. Paris, 1960

Maza, F. de la
Los retablos dorados de la Nueva España. Mexico, 1950

Maza, F. de la
Cartas barrocas desde Castilla y Andalucía. Mexico, 1963

Palm, E.W.
Los monumentos arquitectónicos de la Española. Ciudad Trujillo, 1955

Reyes Valerio, C.
Trilogía barroca. Mexico, 1960

Reyes Valerio, C.
Tepalcingo. Mexico, 1960

Schubert, O.
Geschichte des Barock in Spanien. Esslingen, 1908

Sitwell, S.
Southern baroque art. London, 1927

Sitwell, S.
Spanish baroque art with buildings in Portugal, Mexico and other colonies. London, 1931

Smith, R.C.
A talha em Portugal. Lisbon, 1962

Torres Balbas, L. and others
Resumen histórico del urbanismo en España. Madrid, 1954

Toussaint, M.
Arte colonial in México. Mexico, 1962

Vicens Vives, J.
Historia social y económica de España y América. Barcelona, 1957–1958

Villegas, M.V.
El gran signo formal del barroco. Ensayo histórico del apoyo estípite. Mexico, 1956

Wethey, H.E.
Colonial architecture of Antigua Guatemala. Cambridge (Mass.), 1949

The photographs published on pages 147 and 150, Plaza de Armas and staircase of the Royal Palace of Madrid, are from Jean Dieuzaide, Toulouse (Photo Yan).